The Essentials of First Aid

5TH EDITION

First published in Great Britain in 1987 by
The Order of St. John, Priory House,
St. John's Lane, London EC1M 4DA
071–251 2482

Fourth edition first impression August 1987 44/44035
Second impression (with amendments) May 1989 34/51047
Third impression April 1991 34/57130
Fifth edition November 1992 24/61209

ISBN No. 0 900700 440

St. John Supplies Product R00033

Designed and Printed in England by Lamport Gilbert Limited, Reading

Foreword

This fifth edition of Essentials of First Aid follows the approach of its predecessors in presenting the practices of First Aid in a clear and easily understood way.

The book includes procedures contained in the sixth edition of the joint authorised First Aid Manual published in November 1992.

DR. A. J. BLOWERS, CBE JP DL
Director-General
NOVEMBER 1992   St. John Ambulance

Contents

What is First Aid?

> *First Aid is the skilled application of accepted principles of treatment when injury or sudden illness occur, using facilities or materials available at the time. It is the approved method of treating a casualty until placed, if necessary, in the care of a doctor or removed to hospital.*

The First Aider's responsibility only ends when:

- a doctor, nurse or other responsible person takes over the care of the casualty;
- he or she has given a report to the person in charge and checks whether any further help can be given.

In special circumstances (for example in a sparsely populated area) the First Aider may have to stay with the casualty for several hours. Treatment like redressing injuries and other after-care may then become a responsibility.

The First Aider's role is so important that the general public has a right to expect that such volunteers be:

highly trained;
regularly examined;
kept up-to-date in knowledge and skill.

This emphasis on training has applied since 1894 when the term First Aider was first used by the Voluntary First Aid Organisations.

In this book you will be shown various standard procedures and methods of treatment. You will find, however, that injuries vary and that no two incidents are alike – so you must be prepared to adapt. In real life you may also find that an accident creates more than one injury – it will be your responsibility to decide which needs the most urgent treatment. In other words, alongside the relevant knowledge and skills a First Aider must use Common Sense.

First Aid has four parts:

1. Assessing the situation.
2. Deciding what is wrong with the casualty (diagnosis).
3. Giving immediate and appropriate treatment.
4. Disposing of the casualty – to doctor, hospital or home as appropriate.

1. Assessing the situation:

Your duty is to help the casualty until a more qualified person (such as a doctor) arrives. Here are some guidelines which you should follow:

Appear calm

This will help to give the casualty confidence in you. The person will start to realize that a trained First Aider is there to help.

Take charge

Again this will give the person confidence.

Ensure safety

Of yourself as well as the casualty.

Use bystanders

To telephone the emergency services;
To keep back spectators;
To control traffic;
To help you with actual treatment.

2. Diagnosis:

When you arrive at an incident you may immediately realize what has happened to the casualty – you could tell that a person has fallen or is trapped. Just by using your senses you can get a lot of useful information. If you continue to use your eyes and ears, your touch and sense of smell then you will be able to diagnose more precisely what is wrong.

Listen

Listen to bystanders; what happened? what is the **history** of the case?

Listen to the casualty; what happened? if conscious you should ask tactfully if there is:
pain, loss of sensation, loss of normal movement, weakness, dizziness, faintness, temporary loss of consciousness
or if there are feelings of:
sickness (nausea), thirst, cold or heat.
In other words, what are the **symptoms**?

If the casualty is unconscious then listen to the breathing.

Smell

The person's breath and the surroundings, try to notice:
anything unusual on the breath; burning, gases or alcohol in the area.

Look

Look at the casualty, notice:
breathing, bleeding (type and quantity), colour of face, swelling, deformity, bruising, dampness, vomit, response to your touch or to sound.

At the scene, notice:
containers (bottles, tins, drug packets);
clues carried by an unconscious casualty
(hospital appointment cards, special
warning bracelets or lockets).

Touch

Examine the casualty gently and
carefully. Start at the head and neck,
work down the spine and trunk, check
the arms and finally the legs. Use two
hands and compare the two sides of the
body.

Notice
dampness (bleeding or incontinence),
temperature, pulse, swelling, any
deformity or irregularity, tenderness.

Any unusual things that you have
noticed are the **signs** that something is
wrong.

You may need to loosen or remove
clothing. Be careful, you could worsen a
person's injuries by being rough.

If you do have to take off a jacket, shirt
or vest follow these steps:
Slip the garment over the shoulders.
Bend an uninjured arm and take off that
sleeve first.
Gently slip the other arm out.

If absolutely essential, slit the garment
up the seam on the injured side.

If the thigh is injured, pull trousers
down from the waist. If the calf or knee is
affected, raise that trouser leg to reveal the
injury.

If essential, slit up the inner seam of the
trouser leg.

When taking off shoes, support the
ankle; undo or cut any laces and then
remove the shoe.

If long boots are worn and these will not
undo, carefully slit the back seam.

If socks are difficult to get off, pull the
sock from against the person's leg and cut
it away.

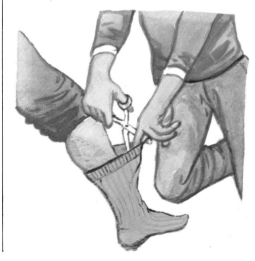

Protective helmets should normally be left on. A full face helmet should **never** be removed unless (i) it obstructs breathing, (ii) the casualty is vomiting or (iii) there are severe head injuries.

If you do decide to remove helmets, follow these guidelines:

Full face helmet – you need two people, one to support the head and neck while the

other tilts the helmet back, lifts it clear of the chin then tilts it forward to clear the base of the skull and then lifts it straight off.

Other helmets – unfasten or cut the chin strap, force the sides apart then lift up and back.

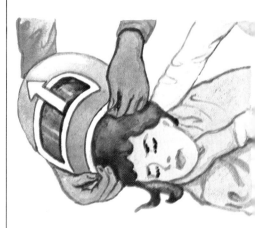

So, using hearing, sight, touch, smell (and common sense) you should find out the history, the symptoms and finally the signs and make your diagnosis.

The common sense aspect is needed, for example, if the casualty is not breathing – you would obviously need to apply Artificial Ventilation as a first priority rather than continuing with an examination.

As you learn about different types of injuries you will be told the symptoms and signs which normally apply. In an unconscious casualty there is one special feature which you should always try to note – that is the casualty's level of responsiveness to you. You will find more detail about that on page 52.

3. Treatment:

First Aid treatment is given:
to preserve life;
to prevent the casualty's condition from becoming worse;
to promote recovery.

Urgent treatment involves these actions:

A make sure that the **airway** is open to let fresh air to the lungs and then keep it open by placing the casualty in the Recovery Position (page 14 and 19).

B if a casualty has stopped **breathing** give mouth-to-mouth ventilation (page 15);

C if the person's **circulation** has stopped (see "carotid pulse" page 14) then apply Chest Compression (page 17).
Control severe bleeding (page 37).

These techniques must be learnt under trained supervision.

Important treatment includes:

- Dress wounds (page 36).
- Support large wounds and fractures.
- Put the casualty in the correct position and make as comfortable as possible in that position.

Helpful treatment includes:

- Calm the person and be sympathetic.
- Reduce pain and discomfort.
- Handle gently so as not to cause more harm or pain.
- Protect from the cold and damp.

4. After treatment:

You must arrange for the casualty's "disposal":
- To hospital.
- To the care of a doctor, nurse or other responsible person.
- To, for example, a nearby house whilst waiting for an ambulance.
- To home (after being told to seek medical advice if necessary). But **do not** send anyone home who has been unconscious (even if only for a short time) or who is badly shocked.

A message explaining the history, symptoms and signs (including levels of responsiveness) and the treatment you have provided should go with the casualty if they are going to hospital or a doctor. If necessary you should accompany the person to make your report.

- Tell a relative, friend, employer, school teacher or anyone else who needs to know about the incident.
- Tell the police about serious outdoor accidents.

Your actions:

To summarize your actions at an incident, follow these steps – in this order:

DO

Eliminate danger to yourself and the casualty.

Act quickly, quietly and calmly.

Give priority to the most urgent conditions.

Check for consciousness

Apply A, B, C – check and, if necessary, deal with airway, breathing, circulation.

Control bleeding.

Check the levels of responsiveness and complete the diagnosis.

Reassure the casualty.

Guard against shock.

Put the person in the correct position and make as comfortable as possible – but **do not** move more than is absolutely necessary.

Remember that the person may have internal bleeding or be poisoned.

Treat large wounds and fractures before moving the person.

Arrange for disposal.

Watch and record any changes in the casualty's condition.

Use your common sense

DO NOT

Try to do too much.

Let people crowd around and get in the way or embarrass the casualty.

Remove or damage clothing unnecessarily.

Give anything to eat, drink or smoke to someone who:
a) is unconscious
b) might have internal injuries
c) might need an anaesthetic.

Attempt to move a casualty with a suspected spinal injury unless life is in danger.

Respiration

Respiration • Asphyxia • Airway • Check Breathing and Circulation • Mouth-to-Mouth • Oxygen and Blood • Chest Compression • Recovery Position • Possible Causes of Asphyxia

RESPIRATION

(or breathing) is the way that we:

- take oxygen from the air into our bodies;
- transfer some of that oxygen into the blood (which carries it round the body);
- remove waste carbon dioxide (which is created when the oxygen is used).

The three stages of breathing in, breathing out and pausing are controlled by a special centre in the brain. What happens is that:

Breathing in:

The ribs are pulled up by the chest muscles.

The diaphragm (which is muscular) tightens and pulls down.

These two movements mean that there is more space in the chest for the lungs (and air inside them) so air is sucked in.

Breathing out:

The rib muscles and diaphragm relax so that there is less space and air is forced out.

There is then a short pause before the process starts again.

ASPHYXIA

is what happens when there is not enough oxygen available to the tissues of the body.

Possible causes include:

Problems of the airway and lungs:

Blocked airway – someone choking
Mouth and nose obstructed – suffocation
Windpipe compressed – someone strangled
Chest compressed – person buried under sand
Lungs injured – car accident
Chest wall injured – person being crushed
Fits – epilepsy, convulsions.

Problems with the control of respiration:

Electrical injury
Poisoning – drug overdose
Paralysis – injury to brain or spine.

Problems of oxygen not going into the blood:

Insufficient oxygen – smoke filled room
Air pressure – going up to extreme heights in a light aircraft.

Problem of body being prevented from using oxygen:

Poisoning – for example, by carbon monoxide in car exhaust fumes.

Symptoms and signs

Breathing:
- Is difficult – rate and depth increase
- Is noisy – snoring or gurgling
- May stop
- Lips and fingernails may be blue.

Person may be:
- Confused
- Unconscious
- Frothing at the mouth.

Treatment

Remove the cause (see examples on pages 20 to 26).

Open the airway (see below).

Check breathing and pulse (see below).

If person is not breathing, but has a pulse, apply artificial ventilation (see page 15).

Apply chest compression if there is no pulse (page 17).

When person is breathing place in recovery position (page 19).

Seek medical help as soon as possible. If there is no pulse and you are on your own, send for an ambulance first, then start treatment. If there is a pulse, give 10 breaths before going for help.

OPENING THE AIRWAY

The airway could be blocked, for example, by an object like a child's toy, by food or drink, by vomit or by an unconscious person's tongue.

Noisy breathing is obstructed breathing.

Remove anything which is obviously in the way – open the airway.

Lift the chin forward with the index and middle fingers of one hand, while pressing the forehead backwards with the heel of the other hand. The tongue will now be lifted forward – clear of the airway.

Remove any obvious items from the mouth that may block the airway.

Do not waste time searching for hidden obstructions.

Opening the airway may in itself be enough to restart breathing.

CHECK BREATHING

Look for movement of the chest and upper abdomen.

Listen and feel for breath on your cheek.

CHECK CIRCULATION

at the carotid pulse.

This is the only reliable way to check whether the heart is beating (the pulse at the wrist is unreliable).

Feel for the pulse in the hollow between the voice box and the muscle in the neck. If there is a pulse, commence mouth-to-mouth ventilation.

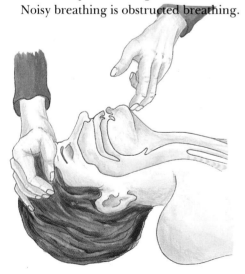

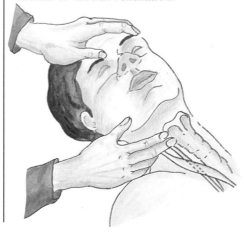

MOUTH-TO-MOUTH VENTILATION

You should normally use this method of getting oxygen into a casualty who is not breathing. It works because the air you breathe out contains a lot of unused oxygen – so you can blow that into the other person.

Action

Clear anything that is obviously in the way and

Open the airway (page 14).

Open your mouth wide, take a deep breath, pinch the person's nostrils together and put your lips around the mouth.

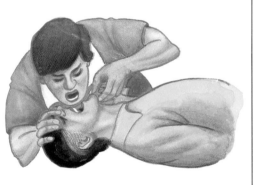

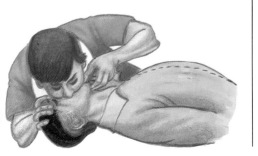

Looking along the chest blow until you see the chest rise fully. (If it does not rise – adjust the open airway. If it still does not rise – treat as choking (page 20).)

Move your mouth away from the casualty and finish breathing out.

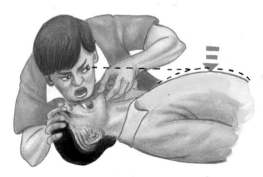

When the casualty's chest falls, take in fresh air and repeat the process.

Continue to breathe for the casualty at about 10 per minute, checking the pulse every 10 breaths, until the person is breathing naturally. Assist breathing if necessary – in other words do some of the breathing for the person.

When breathing normally the casualty should be moved into the recovery position (page 19).

(page 19).

Use your common sense

If the mouth cannot be used, close the mouth with your thumb and blow into the nose.

With a baby, cover the mouth and nose with your mouth and puff gently until the chest rises.

OXYGEN AND BLOOD

The oxygen is carried from the lungs in the red blood cells. This freshly oxygenated, bright red blood pours into the heart and is then pumped out into the main artery from where it is distributed to all parts of the body (body tissues).

Deoxygenated blood flows back from the tissues into the two main veins and then to the heart and back to the lungs.

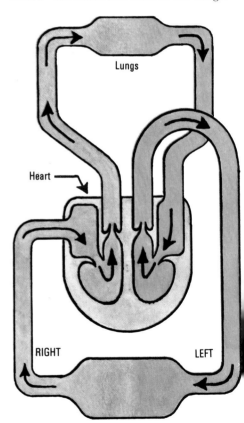

Lungs

Heart

RIGHT   LEFT

Body tissues

If the blood is low in oxygen then blueness may be noticed – particularly in the lips, earlobes and the base of the fingernails.

Paleness (pallor) is caused by a lack of blood in the skin.

If the heart is not beating then oxygen obviously cannot be moved from the lungs to the tissues which need it. You must check that the heart is working (see page 14) – if it is not working, ensure that someone has sent for an ambulance, then use chest compression combined with ventilations.

CHEST COMPRESSION

This does the work of the heart, forcing oxygenated blood out to the different parts of the body. Your hands must be directly above the heart – you then press down following the instructions below.

Action

Lay the person on the back on a firm surface.

Find the junction of the rib margins and the bottom of the breast bone. Put the heel of the hand two fingers breadth above this. You are now in position above the heart and ready to start pumping.

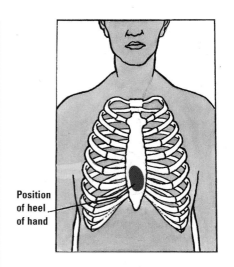

Position of heel of hand

Cover this hand with the heel of your other one, locking your fingers together and keeping them off the chest.

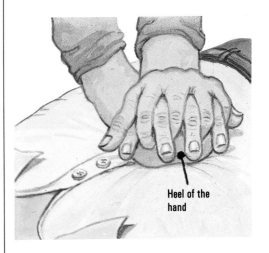

Heel of the hand

Keep your arms vertical pressing down about 4 to 5 cms (1½ to 2 inches) for an adult.

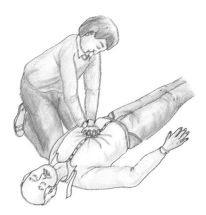

Release the pressure.

Repeat this process fifteen times at a little quicker than once each second (80/minute). Count "one and two and three" and so on to check the time.

Move back to the casualty's head and re-open the airway (page 14) – give two breaths of artificial ventilation slowly one after another allowing the chest totally to deflate between each breath.

Continue with another fifteen compressions, another two breaths.

Keep repeating the fifteen compressions/two breaths cycle.

Use your common sense:
DO NOT WASTE TIME

Children and babies obviously need less pressure for chest compression.

Small Children

Place one hand over the centre of the breastbone. Press down 2·5 to 3·5 cms (1 to 1½ inches) – slightly faster than with adults – do the five compressions (100/minute) then give one ventilation (mouth-to-mouth) at a rate of twenty breaths per minute.

Babies

Use two fingers over the centre of the breastbone – press down 1·5 to 2·5 cms (½ to 1 inch). The rate is again five compressions (100/minute) followed by one ventilation (mouth-to-mouth and nose) puffing gently (rather than blowing) at a rate of twenty puffs per minute.

Use your common sense

TWO FIRST AIDERS

If there are two First Aiders then one should take charge and give mouth-to-mouth ventilation. The other should do chest compression.

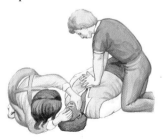

The process is slightly different from when you are alone.

The cycle is:

One breath – five compressions (at 80 compressions per minute).

The next breath is given on the upstroke of the fifth compression. The compressions must carry on after a short pause to allow the lungs to be inflated.

The emergency process for someone who is unconscious is:

A Airway

- Open it by lifting the chin.

B Breathing

- Check whether the casualty is breathing.

C Circulation

- Check carotid pulse.
- If no heartbeat do chest compression and artificial ventilation.
- If there is a pulse do artificial ventilation only.

RECOVERY POSITION

This is a safe position to place an unconscious casualty who is breathing and whose heart is beating.

You must use it if:

Breathing becomes difficult or noisy.

You have to leave the person (for example, to treat another casualty) – **normally you should not leave an unconscious person.**

In the recovery position with the airway open, fluid in the mouth can run out.

Action

Follow these steps:

Kneel beside the casualty, remove any spectacles and straighten the legs. Place the near arm out at right angles to his body, elbow bent, palm uppermost. Bring the far arm across the chest and hold hand, palm outwards, against near cheek. With your other hand, grasp far thigh and pull knee up, keeping foot flat on ground. Keeping his hand pressed against his cheek, pull at thigh to roll him towards you onto his side. Tilt head back to keep airway open and adjust hand under cheek, if necessary, to maintain position. Adjust upper leg if necessary, so that hip and knee are bent at right angles.

Use your common sense

If the person has fractured limbs then you obviously should not move them to act as supports.

Another technique which can be useful is to lay a rolled up blanket under the front of the body to act as a support.

POSSIBLE CAUSES OF ASPHYXIA

DROWNING

CHOKING

ELECTRICAL INJURIES

ASTHMA

WINDING

The general treatment stages for asphyxia are:

Remove the cause.

Open the airway.

Apply artificial ventilation if necessary.

Check the carotid pulse.

Apply chest compression if necessary.

Place a breathing person in the recovery position.

Seek help as soon as possible (send to hospital if necessary).

In the examples listed above those stages should be applied as follows:

Drowning
Symptoms and signs
- As asphyxia (page 13).
- Froth round lips, mouth and nostrils.

Treatment
Carry out general treatment stages for asphyxia (see above) and remove wet clothes. Keep the casualty warm and check and treat for hypothermia (page 100), if necessary.

Remove to hospital.

Choking
Symptoms and signs
- As asphyxia (page 13).
- Cannot speak or breathe.
- Prominent veins in face and neck.

Treatment
Conscious adults:
Open the airway and remove any debris, false teeth and encourage the person to cough.

Help casualty to bend forward with the head lower than the lungs.

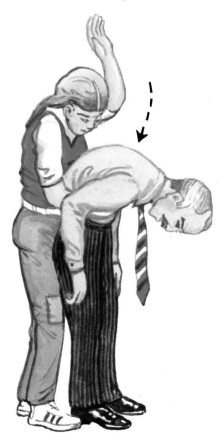

Slap up to five times between the shoulder blades with the heel of your hand. Each slap should be firm enough to dislodge the obstruction.

Check the mouth, if the obstruction is visible then hook it out with your fingers.

If the obstruction has not been dislodged, apply abdominal thrust (this should only be used if essential – it is possible to injure the casualty).

Stand or kneel behind the person with one arm round the abdomen. Clench your fist with the thumb against the casualty, place it in the centre of the abdomen, between the navel and breastbone.

Grasp this fist with your other hand and pull towards you, thrusting upward and inward. Do this up to five times.

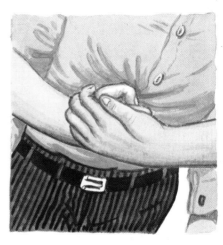

Check the mouth again.

If necessary, repeat backslaps and abdominal thrusts.

If the casualty becomes unconscious go through the following steps.

Treatment
Unconscious adults

Open the airway and apply artificial ventilation (page 15).

If this does not work then pull the casualty onto the side facing you with the chest against your thigh and the head well back.

Slap up to five times with the heel of your hand between the shoulder blades.

Check the mouth.

If the obstruction is still not cleared, put the person on the back – open the airway – kneel astride the thighs (or, if necessary, kneel alongside). Place the heel of one hand in the centre of the casualty's upper abdomen, cover with your other

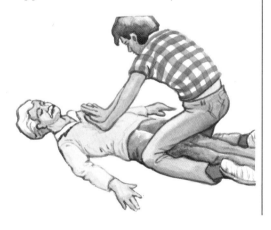

hand. Keep your fingers clear of the abdomen and (with straight arms) give a quick inward and upward thrust.

Do this up to five times – if choking persists then send for an ambulance and start resuscitation.

Treatment
Children

You will be too tall to stand behind so sit down or kneel on one knee with the child head down over the other knee.

Support the chest with one hand and slap between the shoulder blades up to five times.

If necessary, apply the abdominal thrust by sitting the child on your lap. Use one hand with the fist clenched and thumb against the body. Support the back with the other hand. Press in and up with much less pressure than for an adult. Do this up to five times. Only use this technique if you have been trained.

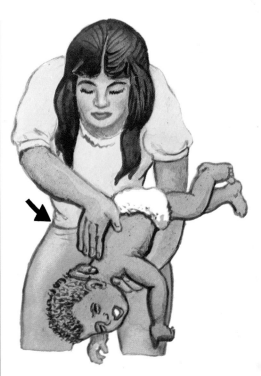

If the child becomes unconscious, follow the stages for an adult (page 22) but when doing the abdominal thrust on an unconscious child use only one hand and less pressure.

Treatment
Infants

Lay the baby face down along your forearm – use your arm to support the head and chest.

Slap smartly between the shoulders up to five times.

Be very careful when checking the mouth – **do not** put your fingers in unless you can see the obstruction and there is no danger of pushing it further down the throat.

Do not apply abdominal thrust on an infant.

In all cases of choking – after the obstruction has been removed:

Apply artificial ventilation if necessary.

If the person has been unconscious remove to hospital.

Otherwise get the person to sit quietly and take sips of water as necessary.

Electrical injuries
Symptoms and signs

- As asphyxia (page 13).
- Shock (page 31).
- Possible burns.
- Possible other multiple injuries.

Low voltage (as in a house)

Action/treatment

Never touch the casualty with bare hands until you have removed the source. Switch off at the mains or meter if it can be quickly reached, otherwise remove the plug or pull the cable free. If you cannot break the electrical circuit in this way then stand on dry insulating material such as wood, a rubber mat or newspaper then use a wooden brush, chair or something similar to push the person from the source. Alternatively (without touching!) loop a dry rope or pair of tights round the legs and pull the person away.

Apply general treatment for asphyxia (page 20) in addition you may need to treat for burns (page 96).

High voltage (powerlines/overhead cables)

These incidents are usually fatal, there are always severe burns and the casualty

may have been thrown from the point of contact by a muscular spasm.

If a casualty is within 18 m (20 yards) of a source, **do not approach or try to rescue** until you have been told by an official that it is safe. The electricity may "arc" and jump considerable distances. Insulating materials will have no practical effect.

Action/treatment

Arrange for the police to be called.

Keep bystanders away from the danger area.

When the authorities have switched off the power and you have been told that it is safe to approach then (if appropriate) apply the general treatment for asphyxia (page 20).

You will also need to treat for burns (page 96).

> # Use your common sense:
> ### Do not turn yourself into another casualty

18 metres (20 yards)

Asthma

Symptoms and signs

- As asphyxia (page 20)

Note: person may be very anxious and have difficulty in breathing out and have blueness of face.

Treatment

Reassure and calm the person.

Get the person to sit down and lean forward resting on a support.

Provide good supply of air.

Let casualty take any medication they have to treat an attack.

Seek medical aid.

Winding

Symptoms and signs

As asphyxia (page 20).

- Difficulty in breathing in
- Difficulty in speaking
- Clutching upper abdomen
- Possible nausea and vomiting.

Treatment

If conscious – get person to sit, leaning forward slightly.

If unconscious – put in recovery position (page 19).

Loosen tight clothing around the neck, chest and waist.

Gently massage the area.

Hiccups

This common complaint is also related to respiration.

Treatment

Get person to sit quietly, hold breath or have long drinks.

Place a paper (**not** plastic) bag over the nose and mouth and get the person to breathe in and out.

If hiccups persist for more than a few hours, seek medical aid.

The St. John Cadets

The St. John Cadets

St. John Ambulance has over 23,000 Cadets throughout England and Wales aged between 10 and 17 years, forming nearly one third of the total membership of St. John Ambulance. To join the organisation recruits complete the Action Pack – a six session induction training programme – to qualify for uniformed membership.

Training

Once members, Cadets undertake training which qualifies them to give service to the community by providing First Aid at public events. But being a Cadet is not only about learning First Aid, it is also about developing skills in a number of areas – communication, leadership, caring, instructional skills, creativity – and having fun.

First Aid and Care

St. John Cadets may accompany Adult members on First Aid Duties, where they get hands-on experience of dealing with the public and putting their First Aid skills into practice. They can help out in hospitals, old people's homes and elsewhere using their skills in caring for the sick. There are also opportunities to take part in competitions linked to First Aid and Care.

The Future

Through their interest in First Aid, many St. John Cadets join the medical and nursing professions and many more go on to University or College. Subjects studied are wide ranging – Aeronautical Engineering, Teacher Training, Business Studies, Linguistics, Environmental Studies and so on. Cadets who leave to go to Higher Education are able to join a St. John Links group – now established in many Colleges throughout the country. This offers the student an opportunity to take part in public service, training courses and exciting social activities.

Why St. John?

Membership of St. John Ambulance offers young people the chance to experience new activities, develop new skills, achieve self confidence, meet people and broaden their experience of life. The Grand Prior Award, the highest award a cadet may achieve, together with other elements of the the St. John Youth programme all contribute to the development of young people as citizens in today's society.

St. John Ambulance, 1 Grosvenor Crescent, London SW1X 7EF.
Tel: 071-235 5231   Fax: 071-235 0796

Circulation and Circulatory Disorders

Circulation • Pulse • Shock • Fainting • Heart Disorders • Coronary Obstruction • Cardiac Arrest • Stroke

CIRCULATION

Oxygen is carried from the lungs in the blood – it is pumped through tubes called arteries, capillaries and veins by the heart.

The heart itself is a muscular organ – each side acts like a pump with valves to make sure that the blood flows in the correct direction. There are four chambers in the heart, a collecting chamber and a pumping chamber on each side.

The heart beats between 60 and 80 times (average 72) a minute in a normal resting adult and faster in a child (100/minute). Every time it beats it forces a surge of blood along the arteries – when these are close to the skin (as in the wrist and neck) a pulse can be felt by pressing the artery gently against the bone on which it lies.

PULSE

The pulse at the neck (carotid pulse) is the most useful for First Aiders. It can be felt just below the angle of the jaw in the hollow between the voice box and the muscle. See comments about carotid pulse on page 14.

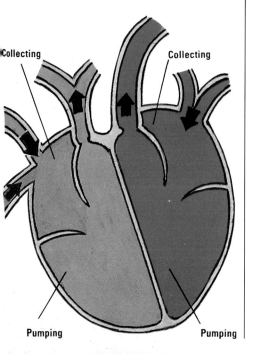

Collecting   Collecting

Pumping   Pumping

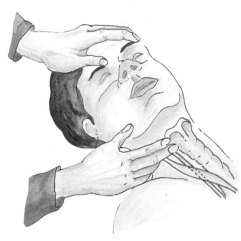

The pulse at the wrist (radial pulse) should be taken with your fingers (not thumb as that has a pulse of its own). Lightly press your finger tips into the hollow at the front of the wrist about 1 cm ($\frac{1}{2}$ inch) from the thumb side of the lower end of the forearm.

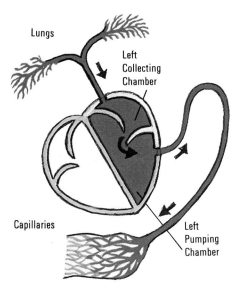

Count the number of beats in 60 seconds and also note the rhythm and strength (is the pulse irregular? is it feeble?).

The pulse can give you a lot of clues – for example a fast, weak pulse might show that an apparently uninjured person has actually got internal bleeding.

A pulse of normal rate and strength shows that the heart is probably doing its job:

taking freshly oxygenated blood from the lungs to the left collecting chamber through to the left pumping chamber where it is pumped out through the strong arteries. These divide and sub-divide until they become tiny capillaries carrying blood to every part of the body.

Other capillaries carry the used blood back towards the veins. The veins carry the blood back to the right collecting chamber of the heart. It then passes through to the right pumping chamber. Here it is pumped to the lungs where it picks up oxygen.

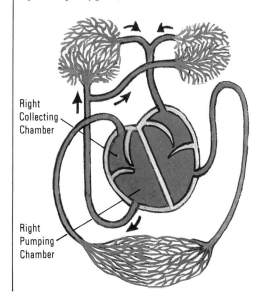

This arrangement of heart and tubes is called the **circulatory system**.

The red colour in blood is given by red cells containing haemoglobin which actually carry the oxygen. There are also white cells (which help remove germs and dead cells) and platelets (which help with clotting) in the blood – all carried in a transparent yellow fluid called plasma. Altogether an average adult would have about 6 litres (10 pints) of blood.

SHOCK

If blood or other body fluid is lost from the circulatory system so that not enough oxygen can be carried to the brain and other parts of the body then a person may suffer from **shock**. This can show itself in different ways (from just going pale to complete collapse or death).

Causes include:

Bleeding (page 35), loss of plasma from major burns (page 94), repeated vomiting or diarrhoea.

Symptoms and signs

- Casualty may feel weak, faint, giddy, frightened, thirsty or sick (and may vomit).
- Skin becomes pale, cold and damp and person may sweat.
- Breathing becomes shallow and fast.
- Pulse rate increases – but is weaker and possibly is irregular.
- The person may yawn or sigh.
- Consciousness may be lost.

Look for clues of an injury which might have caused the shock (you may not be able to rely on what the casualty says.)

Treatment

Immediately reassure and comfort the casualty.

If the casualty's condition allows, lay the person down on the back (on a blanket) with the head low and turned to one side. **Do not** move the person more than you have to.

Raise the legs unless you suspect fractures.

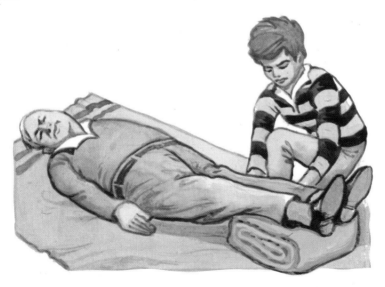

If breathing becomes difficult, person loses consciousness or vomiting seems likely then place in the recovery position (page 19).

Keep the person warm – cover with a blanket or coat but **do not** use a hot water bottle.

Loosen any tight clothing – particularly round the neck, chest and waist.

Search for and, if possible, treat the cause of shock.

If the person is thirsty then moisten lips with water (but **do not** give anything to eat or drink). **Do not** let the casualty smoke.

Check the breathing rate, pulse (page 29) and levels of responsiveness (page 52) at 10 minute intervals.

If breathing stops – apply mouth-to-mouth ventilation (page 14).

If heartbeat stops – apply chest compression (page 17).

Remove to hospital immediately – **DO NOT WASTE TIME.**

FAINTING

This is a brief loss of consciousness caused by the person temporarily not having enough oxygen flowing to the brain.

Common causes include:

Sudden pain;
Sudden fright or other emotion;
Lack of food;
Standing still for a long time.

Symptoms and signs

- As for shock (page 31) **but** the pulse will be **slow** and weak (not fast and weak as with shock) and the person may look very pale.

Treatment

If the person feels unsteady, advise to sit and lean forward with the head between the knees.

Get the person to take deep breaths.

If the person is standing, for example in a crowd or on parade, advise to tighten and relax the leg muscles and move the toes until the circulation improves.

If possible, and always when unconscious – lay the person down, raise the legs and open the airway (page 14) or place in recovery position (page 19).

Loosen any tight clothing round the neck, chest and waist.

See that the casualty has plenty of fresh air, fan air onto the face.

If necessary place in the shade.

Check for and treat any injuries caused by falling.

Check breathing rate, pulse (page 29), and levels of responsiveness (page 52) at 10 minute intervals.

Reassure as the person comes round. Gradually help to sit.

If you are in any doubt about how the person is – get medical help. The person can have sips of cold water (but **not** alcohol) if desired.

HEART DISORDERS

Oxygenated blood can be stopped or hindered from reaching the heart muscles by:

A. **narrowed blood vessels carrying blood for use by the heart tissue itself. (Coronary arteries).**

B. **a blood clot blocking one of these blood vessels.**

Angina pectoris

This is caused by the narrow arteries (A). It is common in elderly people and is usually brought on by exercise or excitement. The attacks normally only last a few minutes. The person may have seen a doctor and know how to cope – for example by resting and/or taking special tablets.

Symptoms and signs

- Pain in chest (often spreading down left shoulder to arm and fingers) – it may also go across the throat and jaw to other arm.
- The skin may be ashen and lips blue.
- The person may be short of breath.
- There is general weakness.

Treatment

Reassure the person.

Help to sit, support by placing a jacket or blanket behind and padding under the knees.

Advise to rest.

Loosen tight clothing around the neck, chest and waist.

If symptoms continue, arrange for removal to hospital.

Heart attack

This is caused by blocked arteries. (B).

Symptoms and signs

- Sudden and extreme crushing pain in the centre of the chest – it may spread to the arms, throat, jaw or back.
- Sudden dizziness causing the person to stop and lean on something for support.
- Ashen skin and blue lips.
- Sweating may develop.
- The person may become breathless.
- Fast pulse becoming weaker and irregular.
- Symptoms and signs of shock (page 31).
- The casualty may become unconscious.
- Breathing and heartbeat may stop.

Treatment

The heart should not be allowed to do any unnecessary work.

You should insist that the casualty does not move at all without help.

If conscious, gently support and place the person in a half sitting position with head and shoulders supported and knees bent.

Loosen tight clothing round the neck, chest and waist.

If the person becomes unconscious but is breathing normally, place in the recovery position (page 19).

If breathing and heartbeat stop, apply mouth-to-mouth ventilation (page 15) and chest compression (page 17).

Treat for shock (page 31).

Check breathing rate, pulse (page 29) and levels of responsiveness (page 52) at 10 minute intervals.

Remove to hospital immediately.

Cardiac arrest

This is when the heart actually stops beating; it can be the result of an extensive coronary obstruction.

Symptoms and signs

- Person becomes unconscious.
- No pulse at the neck (carotid pulse).
- Breathing and heartbeat stop.
- Skin becomes ashen.

Action and treatment

SEND FOR HELP – apply mouth-to-mouth ventilation (page 15) and chest compression (page 17).

Remove to hospital – If necessary, continue treatment on the way.

STROKE

This is another condition which can be caused by a blood clot cutting off the blood supply (this time to the brain). Strokes can also be caused by blood leaking into the brain from a damaged blood vessel.

Strokes are dealt with on page 56.

Wounds and Bleeding

Wounds ● External Bleeding ● Direct Pressure ● Foreign Bodies ● Indirect Pressure ●
Internal Bleeding ● Dressings ● Bandages ● Bleeding from Special Areas

WOUNDS

A wound is an abnormal break in the skin (or any other body tissue) which lets blood escape.

It can be on the outside or the inside of the body (internal bleeding). If the wound is on the outside (external) then germs can get in and cause infection.

EXTERNAL BLEEDING

Types of wound:

Clean cut (incised) – caused by, for example knife or razor blade.

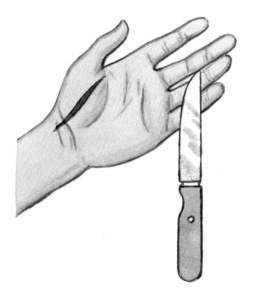

Torn (lacerated) – caused by, for example barbed wire or the claws of an animal.

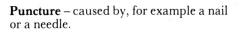

Puncture – caused by, for example a nail or a needle.

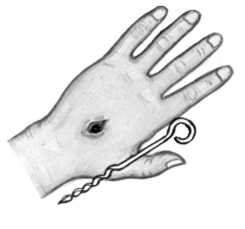

Abrasion – caused by, for example, a sliding fall or friction.

Gunshot – which may have a small entry wound and a large exit wound.

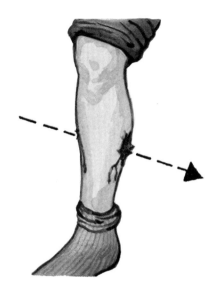

Bruise (contused) – caused by, for example a fall or a punch.

When blood escapes from a damaged blood vessel this is what happens:

The ends of the damaged blood vessels shrink and tighten to make less blood leak out;

The blood pressure drops;

If the wound is large, the smaller blood vessels (which take blood to the skin and muscles) tighten to stop blood flowing to the area. This means that more blood is available for the vital organs.

The blood that has escaped becomes solid so that a clot forms which plugs the damaged vessel and seals the wound.

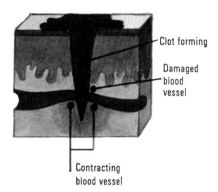

Slight external bleeding – many wounds do not bleed very much and this slight bleeding may soon stop on its own as a clot forms. You can help the process by giving the treatment outlined below.

Treatment

If possible, when dealing with wounds, wash the hands both before and after treating the casualty.

Then, if it is dirty, wash the wound (gently) under running water.

Protect the wound with a sterile swab and carefully clean the surrounding skin with soap and water if available.

Gently wipe away from the wound – take care not to take off any blood clot which is forming. Dab gently to dry. You should use each swab once only (so that you **do not** wipe away a piece of dirt in one movement and then put it back on the wound with the next!).

If bleeding continues:

Apply direct pressure to the wound (page 37).

Dress a small wound with an adhesive dressing (page 40) and a large one with a dressing, pad and bandage (page 41).

Raise and support the bleeding part (page 37) unless you think that there is also a fractured bone (page 61).

If you are in any doubt about the injury, seek medical help.

Major external bleeding is obviously much more dramatic – always check airway (page 14) and breathing before you deal with bleeding. If the bleeding is very severe you may find that you cannot actually stop it – just slow it down. This may still be enough to save the casualty's life.

Treatment

Uncover the wound.

Remove any obvious foreign bodies which can easily be picked out or wiped away.

Apply direct pressure.

Direct pressure

Pressing directly on a wound flattens the blood vessels in the area so that the flow of blood is slowed down. Pressure has to be kept on for 5 to 15 minutes to give the blood time to clot.

Press on the wound, using a dressing if available, with the fingers or palm of the hand or preferably teach the casualty to press himself if he is able.

Lay the casualty down in the most suitable position.

If an arm or a leg is bleeding and there is no fracture (page 61) raise and support it.

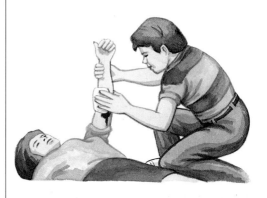

Press a sterile dressing (page 40) onto the wound. Cover with a pad of soft material and hold in place with a firm bandage (page 42). Make sure that the dressing and pad are longer and wider than the wound.

If the wound is large then squeeze the sides together gently but firmly.

Check the circulation (page 38) immediately and at 10 minute intervals.

Symptoms and signs that circulation is affected

- Casualty experiences tingling or lack of feeling in fingers or toes;
- Casualty is unable to move fingers or toes;
- Finger or toe-nail beds are unusually pale or blue;
- Pulse is absent or weak in the bandaged limb (compared with other one);
- Fingers/toes are very cold.

Action to check circulation

Press one of the nails on the bandaged limb until it turns white.

Release the nail and the nail bed should quickly become pink.

If the nail remains white or blue or the fingers are very cold, then the bandage is too tight.

If no pulse can be felt then the bandage is too tight.

If bleeding continues then use another pad on top of the first one. Bandage more firmly (but check circulation). If bleeding still continues apply a third pad and bandage.

Immobilise the injured part.
Treat for shock if necessary (page 31).
Remove to hospital immediately.

If direct pressure still does not stop the bleeding then, as a last resort, apply indirect pressure (page 39).

FOREIGN BODIES FIXED IN WOUNDS

A large object could be helping to plug the wound and cause more damage on the way out **so never try to remove one.**

Treatment

Apply direct pressure by squeezing the edges of the wound together alongside the object.

Gently place a piece of gauze over and around the foreign body.

Put pads of soft material (like cotton wool) around the object until it is high enough to prevent pressure on the object.

Apply a bandage diagonally (page 46) – make sure it is not over the object.

If there is still severe bleeding apply more pads and bandages on top of the original pad. As a last resort use indirect pressure.

Raise the injured part and immobilise.

Treat for shock if necessary (page 31).

Remove to hospital immediately.

Indirect pressure

If the bleeding is very severe and direct pressure does not work (after at least 3 layers of dressings, pads and bandages); or if it is impossible to apply direct pressure then, as a last resort, you should squeeze the actual artery which is supplying blood from the heart. To do that you will need to press it against a bone. The places in the body where you can press an important artery against a bone are called pressure points.

The danger with indirect pressure is that it cuts off all the blood to the arm or leg. **This technique must not be used unless essential. Also, it must not be used for more than 10 minutes.**

Action
Arm

Pass your hand under the person's upper arm and slide your fingers up to near the top. Imagine that you are following the inner seam of a sleeve.

Squeeze your fingers between the muscles, pulling in and up to squash the artery against the bone.

Leg

If possible bend the casualty's knee.

Use your fist or the heel of your hand to press hard down in the centre of the groin to squash the artery against the rim of the pelvis.

INTERNAL BLEEDING

Here the wound is inside the body and you will not see the blood leaking out of blood vessels and you cannot apply direct pressure. The effects of bleeding are just the same; in other words some parts of the body stop getting the oxygen which the blood carries. Always remember that there may be internal bleeding in a casualty involved with a bad accident or if there are symptoms and signs of shock (page 31) but no blood that you can see.

Symptoms and signs

These will vary depending upon how much blood is lost and how quickly.

- History of serious incident.
- History of a medical condition that could cause internal bleeding (for example an ulcer).
- Pain and tenderness around the affected area.
- Symptoms and signs of shock (page 31) – especially if the pulse rate goes on rising despite your treatment.
- Blood may come out of one of the body openings.

Action and treatment

Lay the casualty down with the head down and to one side.

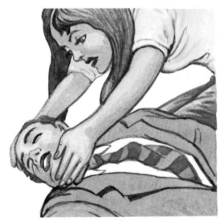

Tell the person not to move.
If possible raise the legs.

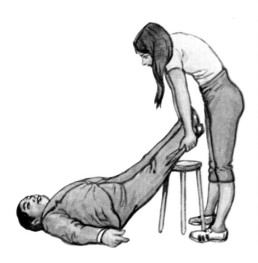

Loosen any tight clothing round the neck, chest and waist.

Reassure the person, explain the need to relax.

Treat for shock (page 31).

Check breathing rate, pulse (page 29) and levels of responsiveness (page 52) at 10 minute intervals.

Examine (page 8) and treat for other injuries (you may not be able to rely on what the casualty says).

If the person becomes unconscious then place in recovery position (page 19).

If breathing and heartbeat stop apply mouth-to-mouth ventilation and chest compression (pages 15 and 17).

Keep the casualty covered and place a blanket underneath if possible (page 106).

If possible keep specimens of anything passed or vomited from the body (if possible send these to the hospital with the person).

Do not give anything to eat or drink.
Remove to hospital immediately.

DRESSINGS

A dressing is a protective cover for a wound, it helps to control bleeding, prevent infection and absorb any discharge.

All dressings should be at least 2.5 cms (1 inch) bigger than the wound.

Dressings should if possible, be sterile so as not to put germs into the wound.

Dressings should be absorbent so that sweat does not make the skin around the wound wet allowing germs to get in.

Types of dressing:
Adhesive dressings or "plasters"
When putting on the wound, make sure that the skin is dry and clean.
NB Some people have skin reactions to adhesive dressings. Enquire before applying.
To use:
Remove the outer wrapping and hold the dressing, gauze side down, by the protective strips.

Peel back, but **do not** remove, the protective strips and, without touching the gauze, place the pad onto the wound.

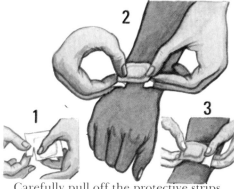

Carefully pull off the protective strips and press the edges down.

Sterile dressings

These are the best First Aid dressings for large wounds. They are sealed in protective wrappers and **should not be used if the wrapping has been broken.**

To use:
Remove both the outer and inner wrappings.

Hold the folded dressing and its special bandage in one hand and unwind the other (short) end of the bandage.

Hold the bandage with the dressing over the wound and open out the folded dressing. Make sure you **do not** touch the side which goes against the wound. Place it on the wound.

Wind the short piece of bandage once round the limb and then bandage firmly with the long piece like a normal roller bandage (page 45).

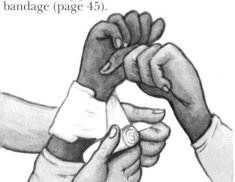

Gauze dressings

These are used where you need a light covering (on a burn for example). If there are no sterile dressings then you

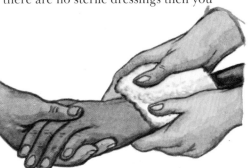

should use one of these with a pad of cotton wool over it. Secure with a bandage or adhesive strapping (page 45).

Use your common sense

Emergency dressings

If a person is capable, ask him to apply direct pressure.

If there are no actual dressings available then use any clean, soft, absorbent material (for example a clean tissue) – held in place by anything that is suitable. **NEVER PLACE FLUFFY MATERIAL (LIKE COTTON WOOL) STRAIGHT ONTO A WOUND**

General rules for applying dressings:

If possible, wash your hands thoroughly before applying dressings.

If a wound is not too large and bleeding is under control, clean it and the surrounding skin (page 37) before applying the dressing (page 40).

Avoid touching the wound or any part of the dressing which will be in contact with a wound.

Never talk or cough over a wound or the dressing.

If necessary cover non-adhesive dressings with pads of cotton wool to help control bleeding and absorb discharge. These pads should extend well beyond the dressing and be held in position with a bandage.

If a dressing slips off a wound before you can fix it in place then use a fresh one – the first one may have picked up germs from the surrounding skin.

Always place a dressing directly onto a wound, **never** slide it on from the side.

BANDAGES

Bandages are used with wounds to:
Maintain pressure over a dressing to control bleeding.
Hold dressings or splints in position.
Prevent swelling.
Provide support for a limb or joint.
Restrict movement.
Occasionally to help lift and carry casualties.
Always check the circulation (page 38) when using bandages.

Types of bandage
Triangular bandage

Made of a piece of material not less than 1 m (1 yd) square cut diagonally

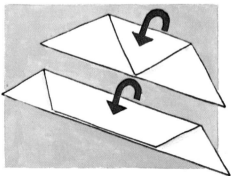

which can be folded into a broad bandage, by folding twice;

or into a narrow bandage by folding the broad bandage in half;

or into an arm sling; (this is covered in detail on page 73).

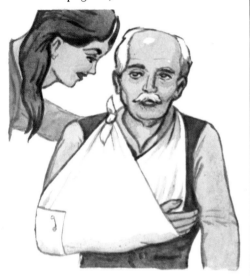

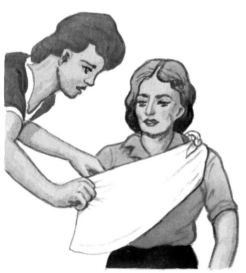

or into an elevation sling; see page 70 for more information.

or into a scalp bandage. Fold the hem of the base and then place that edge across the forehead as shown in the drawing.

Take the two ends round the head and back to the front (tie them with a reef knot).

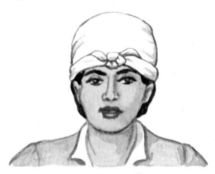

Steady the head and gently draw the point of the bandage down to take up the slack. Now fix that loose point with a safety pin to the bandage on top of the head.

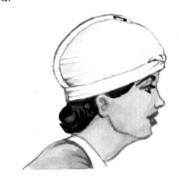

Reef knot:

(In the diagrams one end of the bandage is coloured blue to make the stages clearer.)

Take one end of the bandage in each hand, cross the left end over the right.

Pull that left end underneath and then up.

Turn the ends to face each other.

Cross the end which is now on the right over the left.

Tuck it underneath and then up again.

Pull the knot tight and carefully tuck the ends in.

Make sure that the knot is comfortable, if not place some soft material under it for padding.

Roller Bandage:

This type is available in different sizes – use your common sense – **do not** try to bandage a person's stomach with a 2.5 cms (1 inch) bandage, use a 10 or 15 cms (4 or 6 inch).

How to use:

Before applying a roller bandage make sure it is tightly rolled and of a suitable width.

Place yourself in front of the injury and support the injured part (by hand) where it is to stay.

Keep the main roll (the "head") on top.

Unroll just a short length (5–7·5 cms, 2–3 inches) at a time.

To bandage a left limb, hold the bandage in your right hand. To bandage a right limb, hold the bandage in your left hand.

Always work from the inner side outwards and from below the injury upwards.

Start by making a sharp turn in the bandage so that it will wrap over itself and become fixed.

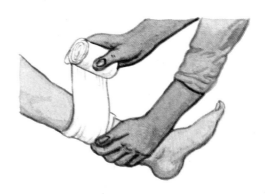

Average Sizes of Roller Bandages for use on Adult Casualties	
Part to be bandaged	Width
FINGER	2.5 cm (1 in.)
HAND	5 cm (2 in.)
ARM	5 or 6 cm (2 or $2\frac{1}{2}$ in.)
LEG	7.5 or 9 cm (3 or $3\frac{1}{2}$ in.)
TRUNK	10 or 15 cm (4 or 6 in.)

Head

Tail

Each of the following turns should cover two-thirds of the previous one.

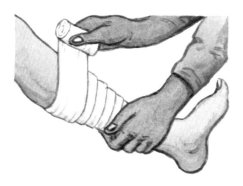

Finish off by turning the end in and fix with a safety pin, adhesive tape or a bandage clip or if none of those is available you should leave about 15 cms (6 inches) of the bandage free and split it.

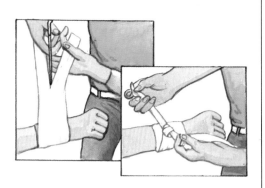

Tie a knot at the bottom of the split and then use the two thin pieces of bandage to hold the rest in place – tying them with a reef knot (page 44).

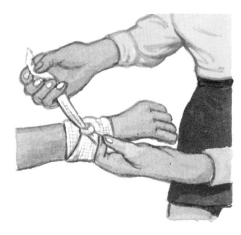

Bandaging round a wound containing a foreign body

You must **not** put any pressure on the foreign body.

Put a piece of gauze over the foreign body and wound.

Place pads of soft material round the object and build up the padding until it is high enough to prevent pressure.

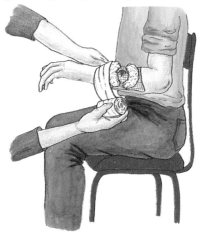

Place the tail of a roller bandage directly under the lower edge of the padding, make two straight turns to fix the bandage in place.

Wind the bandage diagonally across under the limb and then up over the upper part of the padding. Keep bandaging above and below the padding.

The general treatment for wounds is therefore to:

If possible wash the hands before treating.

Apply direct pressure using dressing if available.

Elevate the limb.

Apply pads and bandages (which should stop the bleeding).

As a last resort apply indirect pressure to stop the bleeding.

Immobilise and raise the injured part.

Seek medical help if necessary.

Where possible clean up and wash the hands after treating.

BLEEDING FROM SPECIAL AREAS

Scalp

The skin across the scalp is stretched very tightly so if it is cut (for example in a fight or an accident) the skin splits. There will probably be a lot of blood because there are many blood vessels in the scalp.

Treatment

Do not apply heavy direct pressure if you think there may be a fracture (page 61) or if there is a foreign body in the wound.

Otherwise:

Control the bleeding using direct pressure (page 37).

Place a dressing and pad over the wound (page 41) and apply a scalp bandage (page 43) (remember that a scalp bandage will only hold a dressing in place – not apply pressure).

If the casualty is conscious – lay the person down with the head and shoulders slightly raised.

Check breathing rate, pulse (page 29) and levels of responsiveness (page 52) at 10 minute intervals.

If the person becomes unconscious – place in the recovery position (page 19) with the injured side uppermost.

If breathing or heartbeat stop – begin mouth-to-mouth ventilation and chest compression (pages 15 and 17) **immediately**.

Remove to hospital straight away. **All** head injuries should be looked at by a doctor.

Bleeding from ear

Bleeding from inside the ear canal means that the person must be removed to hospital.

Treatment

Place a conscious casualty in a half-sitting position with the head leaning towards the injured side.

Cover the ear with a sterile dressing or pad (page 40). Bandage gently to hold the dressing in place.

Do not plug the ear or try to stop the blood coming out of the ear.

Check breathing rate; pulse (page 29) and levels of responsiveness (page 52) at 10 minute intervals.

If the person becomes unconscious but is breathing normally, place in the recovery position (page 19), with the head on the injured side to let fluid drain.

If breathing and heartbeat stop apply mouth-to-mouth ventilation (page 15) and chest compression (page 17).

Remove to hospital.

Nose-bleeds

These are common and can occur after a punch, sneezing or simply blowing or picking the nose. There is a danger of the person swallowing or breathing-in blood.

If the liquid is clear watery cerebrospinal fluid, seek medical help (page 55).

Treatment

Get the person to sit with the head forward.

Loosen any tight clothing round the neck and chest.

Get casualty to breathe through the mouth and pinch the soft part of the nose firmly for about 10 minutes – repeat if necessary.

Advise not to swallow any blood.

Do not let the person lift the head.

Do not plug the nose but clean round the mouth and nose.

When the bleeding stops tell the casualty:

Not to blow the nose for at least an hour.

To get medical help if bleeding starts again.

If the bleeding does not stop in half-an-hour seek medical help.

Mouth wounds and bleeding tooth socket

Mouth wounds are usually caused by the person's teeth during, for example, a fall.

Severe bleeding may occur because there are many blood vessels.

Treatment

Get the person to sit with the head tilted forward and towards the injured side.

Mouth wounds:

Control bleeding by placing a clean dressing over the wound and squeezing.

Tooth socket:

Place a thick pad of gauze or cloth on (not in) the socket. Tell the person to hold the pad in place then bite on it for 10–20 minutes.

Tell the person not to swallow blood.

If the wound is large or is still bleeding after 10–20 minutes remove to hospital.

Do not wash the mouth out.

Tell the person to avoid hot drinks for at least 12 hours.

If the person has lost a tooth dental help is needed as soon as possible. If you find the tooth, send it with the casualty.

Palm of hand

Dramatic bleeding can occur when the hand is cut.

There may be additional injuries (see fractures (page 61)).

Treatment

Apply direct pressure unless you think there is a fracture or unless there is something fixed in the wound (if so, follow the steps on page 38). Use a sterile dressing or gauze and pad.

Get the person to squeeze the pad onto

the wound (if it is not possible to move the fingers then get the casualty to use the other hand to close the injured fist and hold the pad in place).

Raise the injured arm.

Bandage the fist (use the ends of the dressing or a broad bandage).

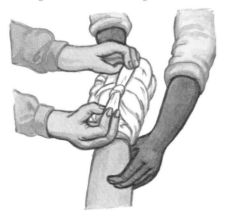

Tie at the knuckles with a reef knot (page 44). Tuck the ends away neatly.

Support the arm in an elevation sling (page 70).

Varicose veins

Some people have a medical problem that causes some of the veins in their legs to collect large amounts of blood. If these varicose veins are injured or get so full that they burst, severe bleeding occurs.

Treatment

Expose the wound immediately.

Get the person to lie on the back and raise the leg as high as possible.

Apply direct pressure (see page 37).

Remove any tight clothing (for example stockings).

Place a sterile dressing (page 41) over the wound. Tie bandage firmly to control bleeding – but do not fix it too tightly.

Check circulation (page 38).

If the dressing becomes soaked then apply fresh ones on top (page 38).

Keep the leg raised and supported.

Treat for shock (page 31).

Remove to hospital.

Animal bites

Any bite causing a break in the skin gives the chance of infection.

Tetanus and, outside the United Kingdom, rabies are dangers.

Action and treatment

Slight bleeding:

Wash wound with soapy water for 5 minutes and apply dressing (page 41).

Seek medical help.

Severe bleeding:

Apply direct pressure (page 37).

Dress the wound (page 40).

Remove to hospital.

Report dog bites to the police.

Bruising

This is one very common form of internal bleeding.

The colour of a bruise is caused by blood from damaged blood vessels seeping through the tissues under the skin.

Symptoms and signs

- Pain and swelling.
- Bluish-purple colour.
- If a bruise shows an outline of, for example clothes, a tyre tread or a boot, it might be a sign of serious internal injuries.

Treatment

Raise the injured part and place in most comfortable position. Apply a cold compress, or ice bag (page 116 and 117) as soon as possible.

Seek medical help if you think there may be internal injuries.

Summary

With bleeding the two main stages in controlling blood loss are:

Applying pressure on the wound if possible (page 37) and reducing the flow (normally by raising the injured part).

Internal bleeding might only show itself by symptoms and signs of shock – (page 31) especially an unexpected increase in pulse rate after treatment. It is just as dangerous as external bleeding.

At an incident the priorities are

Airway

Breathing

Circulation

A B C

and then deal with bleeding. Examine the person as described on pages 8 to 10.

Nervous System and Unconsciousness

**Nervous System ● Levels of Responsiveness ● Examination ● Head Injuries ● Stroke ●
Epilepsy ● Diabetes**

NERVOUS SYSTEM

The nervous system carries messages to
and from every part of the body. These
messages:

Control our movements (for example the
brain "tells" the hand to pick up a pen),
and
Control body functions (for example the
brain keeps "telling" the heart to beat).

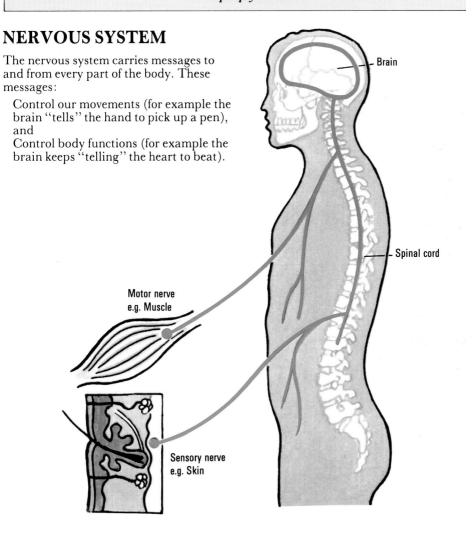

Brain

Spinal cord

Motor nerve
e.g. Muscle

Sensory nerve
e.g. Skin

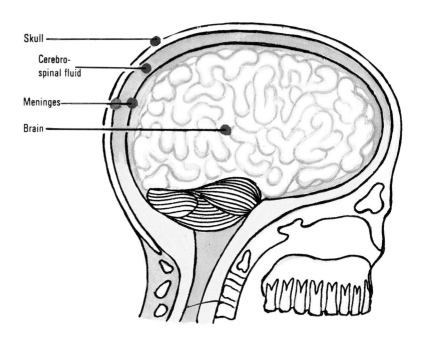

We use the brain to organise things, to tidy up the jumble of messages from our eyes and ears and other senses. The brain must then send out its orders to the different parts of the body.

Those messages travel down the spinal cord and out through nerves to the particular part. If a "motor" part of the nerve is damaged then the message from the brain will not get through and so, for example, the arm or leg will not move.

Messages to the brain travel up the "sensory" part of the nerve and through the spinal cord. If a sensory nerve is injured then the brain will not get a message that there is pain or heat or other sensation.

LEVELS OF RESPONSE

The working of the brain can be tested by measuring the "levels of response" to what is happening. Unconsciousness or partial consciousness show that the brain is not working normally. A casualty will give different signs depending upon these "levels of response".

Assessment of Level of Response

The assessment of the level of response is based on the Glasgow Coma Scale which is internationally recognised and is in use in most hospitals throughout the United Kingdom. It is based upon eye opening, verbal and motor responses, and is a practical means of monitoring changes in the level of consciousness.

What follows is a simplified version of this method of assessment for first-aiders.

Note the time and response to the following:

Eyes – are they open?
> do they open – on command?
> in response to pain?
> e.g. pinching skin on back of hand.
> do they remain closed?

Movement – does casualty move –
> on command?
> in response to painful stimulus?
> make no response?

Speech – is response to question and conversation normal?
> is casualty confused?
> does casualty – use inappropriate words?
> make incomprehensible sounds?
> make no response?

Remember that the casualty may not stay on just one level – he may become less responsive.

EXAMINATION

When you examine the casualty (page 8) you will try to find out why the person has become unconscious – **but do not forget that your first priority is to preserve life**.

You can give adequate treatment to an unconscious casualty without knowing exactly what is wrong with them, although this is helpful and sometimes obvious.

You may be able to get information from a bystander but a casualty who is unconscious will not be able to tell you all the symptoms experienced – so you must be even more careful when looking for signs. When examining an unconscious casualty, follow these guidelines:

Quickly check that the airway is open (page 14) and the the casualty is breathing. If not, start mouth-to-mouth ventilation immediately (page 15). Check circulation (page 19) and control severe bleeding (page 37).

Do not move the person unless breathing is difficult or noisy – if it is then place in the recovery position (page 19).

Move the person as little as possible and be gentle.

Quickly examine over and under the casualty (starting at the head and working

down to the feet) to see if there is serious bleeding which needs urgent treatment. Dampness is the sign that you are looking for.

Now carefully examine the person to find out the cause of unconsciousness.

Check:

Breathing – rate and depth
Pulse – rate and strength
Face and skin – colour, temperature and condition
Head – for injury
Ears, eyes, nose and mouth – for blood or other signs
Whole body – for signs of injury. In particular examine the neck and spine.

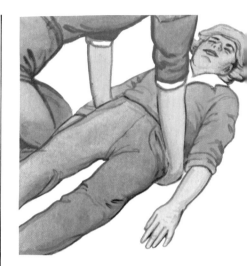

Neck

Loosen clothing round the neck and (very gently and carefully) run your fingers down the spine to between the shoulders. Are there any signs of a fracture? (page 61).

Feel and look round the neck. Is there a special warning medallion? Check the carotid pulse. Is the rate and strength normal? (page 29).

Spine

Do not move the casualty or remove any clothing, but feel (gently and carefully). Is there any swelling? Does anything feel unusual?

Also look out for clues such as warning cards, hospital appointment cards or special lockets and bracelets.

> ## Use your common sense

Stop the examination and deal with airway, breathing or circulation (pages 14 to 19) if you need to.

If at any stage during the examination breathing becomes difficult, with great care place in the recovery position (page 19).

Do not try to move anyone unless you absolutely have to.

Casualties with possible spinal injuries must not be moved unless life is at risk. (See airway page 14, breathing pages 14 and 19, and circulation page 17).

General treatment of unconsciousness

Open the airway (page 14), remove any loose dentures or teeth and clear the mouth of vomit or blood.

Loosen tight clothing around the neck, chest and waist.

Apply mouth-to-mouth ventilation/chest compression if needed (pages 15 and 17).

Treat serious wounds (page 37) and fractures (page 62).

Check breathing rate, pulse (page 29) and levels of response (page 52) at 10 minute intervals and record any observations.

If the casualty is breathing adequately, place in recovery position (page 19).

Cover the person with a blanket and (if possible) place one underneath.

Do not give an unconscious casualty anything by mouth.

Never leave an unconscious casualty alone.

Remove to hospital.

If the person recovers consciousness

Talk calmly, explain what is happening, reassure and advise to see a doctor.

Do not let the casualty have anything to eat, drink or smoke.

If thirsty just moisten the lips with water.

Do not leave the casualty alone (the person could become unconscious again).

There are many injuries which could cause unconsciousness, they include:

Head injuries
Strokes
Epilepsy and
Diabetes.

HEAD INJURIES

These may cause damage to the brain.

There are two possible types of damage to the brain which could make the casualty unconscious; concussion and compression.

Concussion

This might be the result of a fall or another incident which is "brain-shaking".

Symptoms and signs

- Brief or partial loss of consciousness (sometimes the casualty will not even remember it).
- While recovering the person may feel nauseated or already be vomiting.
- When conscious the person may have forgotten what happened just before and after the incident.
- If unconsciousness carries on, suspect **compression.**

Treatment

Carry out the general treatment for unconsciousness (page 54).

Watch for signs of compression.

Remove to hospital immediately.

Compression

This is where there is pressure on the brain (caused by blood taking up space inside the skull or by a skull fracture, see page 64). Concussion can lead into compression.

Symptoms and signs

- **Levels of response fall as compression develops.**
- Breathing becomes noisy.

- Body temperature might rise.
- Face is flushed but dry.
- Pulse is slow, full and bounding (unusually strong).
- May be weakness or paralysis on one side of the body.

Treatment

Carry out the general treatment for unconsciousness (page 54).

Remove to hospital immediately.

STROKE

This can be caused by a blood clot blocking a blood vessel to the brain. Another cause is internal bleeding into the brain.

Symptoms and signs

- There may be symptoms and signs of compression (page 55) but the history may include a mention of high blood pressure.
- Another possible difference is that there is no sign of an injury.
- The person may also have loss of power or sensation in an arm or leg, and the speech may be slurred.

Treatment

Carry out the general treatment for unconsciousness (page 54).

Remove to hospital immediately.

EPILEPSY

This is the result of problems with the normal electrical activity of the brain. There are two types – **minor** and **major**. People who are epileptic may carry an identification card or wear a warning bracelet.

Minor epilepsy
Symptoms and signs

- Casualty appears to be daydreaming staring blankly into the distance.
- The person might start to behave strangely (for example fiddling with clothing, or saying odd things).
- There may be loss of memory.

Action and treatment

Keep the person safe (for example, away from roads).

Keep other people away.

Talk calmly and quietly to the person.

Stay with the casualty until the person has recovered and can get home.

Advise to see a doctor.

Watch for symptoms and signs of a major fit which might follow.

Major epilepsy
Symptoms and signs

- Casualty suddenly loses consciousness and falls to the ground sometimes with a strange cry.
- The person stiffens for a few seconds.
- The face is blue and congested.

If possible, loosen clothing round the neck and place something soft under the head.

Do not move the person unless there is danger.

Do not try to hold the person down.

Do not put anything in the mouth or try to open it.

- Then various muscles make the body jerk about by relaxing and then tightening again.
- Breathing may become noisy or difficult and froth may appear at the mouth (this could be bloodstained if the lips or tongue have been bitten).
- The person may lose control of the bladder or bowel.
- The muscles will then relax.
- The person will stay unconscious for a few minutes or more.

When the jerking movements (convulsions) have finished, place the person in the recovery position (page 19).

Do not try to wake the person.

Stay with the person until you are sure the casualty has recovered completely.

Do not give the person a drink until fully conscious.

Advise the person to tell the doctor of this attack.

Do not send for an ambulance unless the casualty has another attack (fit); has been injured during the fit or takes longer than 10 minutes to recover full consciousness.

- The casualty will then start to regain consciousness but may feel dazed or confused and still be acting strangely (and may want to rest quietly or sleep).
- The person may carry an orange card or wear a warning bracelet.

Action and treatment

Try to help the person down if falling.

Clear spectators away.

DIABETES

Diabetic people need to control their blood sugar level carefully by balancing the amount of sugar in their diet with their medicine (insulin injections or tablets).

A diabetic person may become unconscious due to too much insulin; not enough food or unaccustomed exercise which burns up sugar.

Symptoms and signs

- The person may carry a special card or wear a warning bracelet.
- The diabetic might feel faint, dizzy and know what is wrong.
- The person could be confused and aggressive (as though drunk).
- The face becomes pale.
- The skin may be cold and clammy.
- The pulse is strong and bounding.
- Breathing is shallow.
- Arms and legs start to tremble.
- The level of response (page 52) may go down rapidly.

Treatment

Speed is essential, a brain cannot survive without sugar just as it cannot survive without oxygen.

If the person is conscious and can swallow

immediately give:

Sugar lumps or sugary drink
Chocolate, or
Anything else that is sugary.

Be careful – many modern foods contain artificial sweeteners which will not work.

If the person is unconscious (but breathing normally)

Place in the recovery position (page 19) and carry out the treatment on page 54.

Remove to hospital immediately.

Injuries to Bones

Bones ● Fractures ● Special Fractures ● Elevation Sling ● Arm Sling

BONES

Do various jobs:

They support the body, all the bones together (the skeleton) making us the shape we are;

They protect other parts of the body (for example the skull protects the brain) and

They let us move (giving the muscles, (page 82), something to fix to).

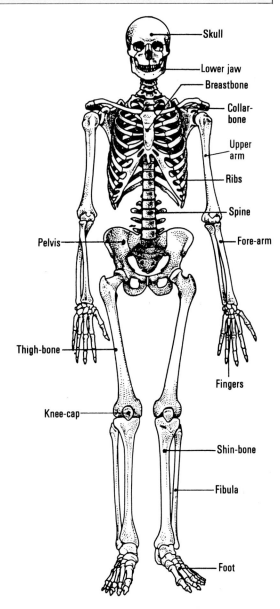

Skull
Lower jaw
Breastbone
Collar-bone
Upper arm
Ribs
Spine
Fore-arm
Pelvis
Thigh-bone
Fingers
Knee-cap
Shin-bone
Fibula
Foot

FRACTURES

A fracture is a broken or cracked bone –
any bones could be fractured but there
are ones which seem more likely to break
(or which are special for some other
reason).

These are marked on the drawing of
the skeleton:

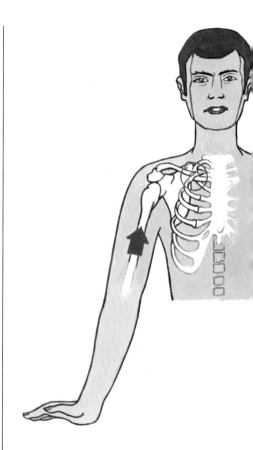

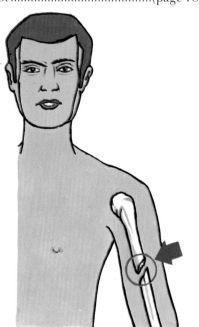

You could find, however, that the injury
happened to a **different** part, for example
someone could fall onto the hand and
actually break the collar-bone, or they
could kick a ball, miss and break a bone in

When examining the casualty you may
find that a fracture has been caused by an
injury to that particular part of the body.
(**Direct force**).

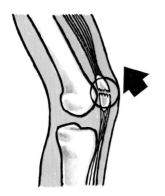

the knee by jerking the muscles or ligaments. (**Indirect force**).

There are two types of fracture:

Closed where only the bone is injured.

Open where the bone has gone through the skin or there is a wound leading to the fracture.

An open or closed fracture is said to be **complicated** when there is another injury to that part of the body. For example, a broken bone which damages a nerve, large blood vessels or body organ, or where a fracture is associated with a dislocation.

Diagnosis

Not all these symptoms and signs will be present in every fracture. When examining the casualty **do not** move any part unless you have to. Compare the two sides of the body to help you notice anything unusual.

If you are in any doubt – **treat as a fracture.**

You must remember that when a bone is broken the surrounding blood vessels and small nerves will also be torn and damaged.

General symptoms and signs

You may find that:

- The snap of the bone was felt or heard by the casualty;
- There is pain at or near the fracture which is increased by movement;
- The person cannot move the part normally;
- There is tenderness on gentle pressure;
- There is swelling and, later, bruising;
- The area looks odd, for example a foot is at a strange angle (deformity).
- There will also be symptoms and signs of shock (page 31) particularly with fractures of the thigh bone and pelvis.
- Special fractures have other symptoms and signs (pages 64 to 78).

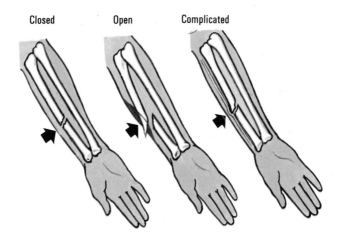

Closed   Open   Complicated

General treatment

Check airway (page 14), breathing and circulation (page 19).

Treat severe bleeding (page 37).

Treat unconsciousness (page 54).

Do not move the person unless you have to.

Steady and support the injured part with your hands above and below the fracture site until it is immobilised.

Use rolled-up blankets or similar things (for example coats) to support the person and the injury.

If removal to hospital is likely to be delayed. Stop the injured part from moving by fixing it to another part of the body with padding and bandages (as described in the examples on pages 64 to 78). Bandages should be firm enough to stop movement but not so tight that they stop the circulation or cause pain (page 38).

Raise the injured part after immobilising it to minimise discomfort and swelling.

If the casualty is to be transported by first aiders, extra bandages and splints may be needed.

Treat for shock (see page 31).

*Note. Normally, young people do not have the responsibility for transport.

Treating an open fracture

If the bone is showing outside the wound.

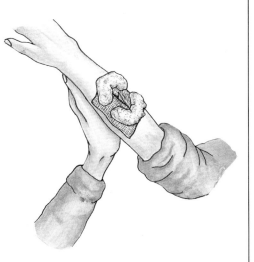

Treat as wound with a foreign body, (page 46) but avoiding pressure on the underside of the fracture.

If possible, raise the injured part and immobilise it.

Remove the person to hospital.
If the bone is not showing:

Control bleeding by squeezing the sides of the wound together gently but firmly.

Use your common sense:
Do not apply direct pressure on the fracture

Place a dressing over the wound (page 46).

Put pads of cotton wool around the edge of the wound.

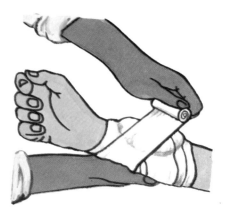

Bandage the wound diagonally.
Raise the injured part (if possible).
Immobilise the fracture.
Remove to hospital.

SPECIAL FRACTURES
Skull

Any head injury is serious – particularly a fracture which damages the brain with clouding or loss of consciousness (page 55).

The outside of the skull could be fractured by, for example, a fall directly onto the head.

The base of the skull could be fractured by indirect force (page 60) (like a punch on the jaw or a fall when the person lands on the feet).

Symptoms and signs

- Obvious signs of a head injury.
- Blood and/or clear cerebro spinal fluid coming from the ear or nose.
- One or both eyes may be "bloodshot" (the white part looks red), later, there may be a black eye.
- The pupils of the eyes may be different in size.
- The casualty may lose consciousness (page 52).

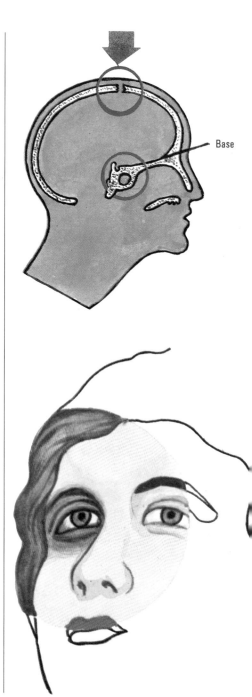

Base

Treatment

If the person is conscious, place in a half-sitting position with the head tilted to the bleeding side. If any fluid comes from the ear, cover it with a sterile dressing and fix gently with a bandage. **Do not** plug the ear.

If unconscious, place in the recovery position, bleeding ear down.

Check the breathing rate, pulse (page 29) and level of response (page 52) at 10 minute intervals.

If breathing and heartbeat stop, apply mouth-to-mouth ventilation (page 15) and chest compression (page 17) **immediately**.

Treat for shock (page 31).

Remove to hospital immediately.

Lower jaw

This is usually due to a direct blow on the jaw. Normally only one side is affected.

Symptoms and signs

- Pain which gets worse if the jaw moves (for example when swallowing).
- Difficulty in speaking.
- The casualty might feel nauseated.
- Person may dribble (and the saliva will probably be blood stained).
- There could be a wound inside the mouth.
- Swelling, tenderness and, later, bruising of the face and lower jaw.

- The underside of the jaw may feel uneven.
- The line of the teeth may also look uneven.

Treatment

Gently open the airway – remove false or loose teeth.

Control bleeding (page 48) and treat any wounds.

If the person is conscious and is not seriously injured then sit the casualty up with the head well forward to let fluid flow out of the mouth.

Support the jaw with a soft pad – get the casualty to hold it in place.

If vomiting occurs support the person's jaw and gently clean out the mouth.

If the casualty is unconscious and breathing normally, put in the recovery position (page 19), with the hand keeping the weight off the jaw.

A casualty with a severely injured jaw should be transported in the recovery position, even if the casualty is conscious.

If breathing and heartbeat stop then use artificial ventilation (possibly mouth-to-**nose**) (page 16) and chest compression (page 17).

Remove to hospital immediately.

Spine

A fractured spine is a serious injury because of the danger of damage to the spinal cord (page 54).

The spine can be fractured by direct force (for example when a person is hit by a car) or by indirect force when the spine is jarred (for example, someone falling and landing on their feet). A common type of neck injury is "whiplash" when the head suddenly moves back (for example when a person is sitting in a car when it hits, or is hit by, another vehicle).

Two parts of the spine which are very likely to be injured are at the neck and the lower back.

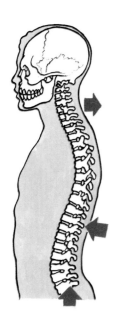

Symptoms and signs

- The casualty may feel severe pain in the back and may feel "cut in half".

- The person might not be able to move the limbs – ask to try to move wrists, fingers, ankles and toes.
- The person might not be able to feel anything – gently touch the hands and legs (without the casualty knowing) and ask if anything is felt.
- Fracture of the spine should always be suspected if the casualty complains of neck or back pain after a serious accident.

Treatment

YOU MUST NOT MOVE THE PERSON UNLESS LIFE IS AT RISK see airway, breathing (page 14); circulation (page 17).

Tell the casualty **not** to try to move.

Keep the head steady by hand. Ask a bystander to support the feet **without** moving them.

Place rolled up clothing alongside the person to support.

Cover with blankets or coats (a casualty with spinal injuries must be kept warm).

Wait for medical help to arrive.

Wait for medical help to arrive.

Rib and breastbone

Rib fractures are usually caused by a fall or a blow to the chest.

Symptoms and signs

- General symptoms and signs of a fracture (page 61).
- Casualty may feel a sharp pain which increases if the person coughs or breathes deeply.
- There may be symptoms and signs of internal bleeding (page 39).
- There may be symptoms and signs of asphyxia (page 13).

Treatment

Support the arm on the injured side in an arm sling (page 73). Remove to hospital.

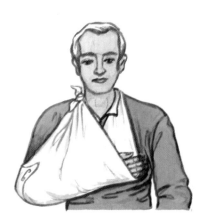

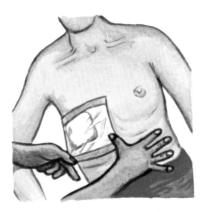

If there are complications with breathing then:

Treat any "sucking" wound of the chest (page 117) by gently placing a sterile dressing over it and try to make an airtight seal by covering the dressing with a piece of plastic or metal foil, and sealing the edges with adhesive ("sticky") tape and/or a bandage.

Lay the casualty down in a half-sitting position with the head and shoulders supported and the body leaning towards the injured side. Support the person by placing a folded blanket along the back.

Support the arm on the injured side in an elevation sling (page 70).

If the casualty is unconscious or breathing becomes noisy and, or difficult

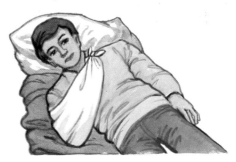

then place in the recovery position (page 19) with the uninjured side uppermost.

Remove to hospital.

Collar-bone

A collar-bone fracture is usually caused by indirect force (for example a fall onto an outstretched hand).

Symptoms and signs

- General symptoms and signs of a fracture (page 61).
- Pain and tenderness at the site of the injury which gets worse when the arm moves.
- The person is unwilling to move the arm.
- The casualty may support the arm at the elbow and keep the head tilted towards the injury (to ease the pain).
- Swelling or deformity may be seen or felt.

Treatment

Gently place the arm on the injured side across the person's chest (the fingertips should be almost resting on the other shoulder).

Support the limb in an elevation sling. Place a broad bandage (page 42) over the sling – tie at front on the uninjured side with a reef knot (page 44).

Remove to hospital.

ELEVATION SLING

This sling is used to support the hand and forearm for shoulder injuries, complicated chest injuries or if the hand is bleeding.

Action

Ask the person to sit with the forearm across the chest – fingertips almost touching the other shoulder.

Place a triangular bandage over the forearm and hand – with the point reaching well beyond the elbow and the upper end on the uninjured shoulder.

Support the forearm and ease the base of the bandage underneath the hand, arm and elbow.

The knot should be in front of the hollow on the uninjured shoulder – just above the collar-bone.

Tuck the point of the bandage between the forearm and the front of the sling. Turn the fold back against the arm and secure with a safety pin.

Take hold of the lower end of the bandage and bring it round the person's back and over the front of the uninjured shoulder.

Gently adjust the height of the sling if necessary and tie the two ends together with a reef knot (page 44).

Check the circulation (page 38) – if necessary adjust the sling slightly.

Use your common sense

If you do not have a triangular bandage then use something else to support the injury, see page 74 for some ideas.

Arm

A fracture can occur anywhere along the arm but a break at the wrist is very common. With children, a fracture involving the elbow joint is again quite common (and this will probably be complicated by injuries to blood vessels and nerves); the circulation in the limb must, therefore be checked (page 38).

Symptoms and signs

- General symptoms and signs of a fracture (page 61).
- Pain at the site of the fracture which gets worse when the arm is moved.
- Casualty is unable to use the injured arm.
- If the elbow is injured then it cannot be bent.

Treatment

Gently support the injured arm across the chest – place soft padding between the arm and chest.

Use an extra fold of padding if the wrist or forearm is hurt.

Support the limb and padding in an arm sling (see below).

Place a broad bandage (page 42) over the sling – tie it at the front on the uninjured side with a reef knot (page 44).

Remove to hospital.

If the elbow cannot be bent:

Treatment

Lay the person down and place the injured arm by the side.

Do not try to bend the elbow.

Get the person to hold the arm in that position if possible.

Place soft padding between the injured arm and the body.

Fix the arm to the body with three broad bandages:

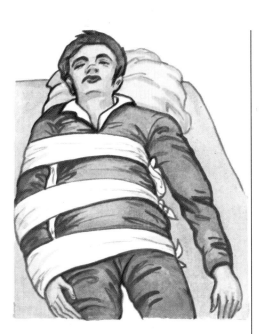

Slide one end of a triangular bandage between the chest and the forearm and then up over the shoulder on the uninjured side, round the back of the neck and over the other shoulder.

Make certain that the point is well beyond the elbow on the injured side.

Still supporting the arm that is hurt, bring the lower end of the bandage up over the hand and forearm.

– around the wrist and hips;
– around the upper arm and chest and
– around the forearm and trunk.

Remove to hospital on a stretcher.

ARM SLING

This holds the forearm across the chest if the person stands or sits.

It is used for arm (and some chest) injuries.

When in the correct position:
– the hand will be slightly higher than the elbow; and
– the fingernails will be showing.

Action

Ask the casualty to sit down – if possible get them to support their arm with the wrist and hand a little higher than the elbow – otherwise you should support it.

Tie the two ends together with a reef knot (page 44) (this should fit into the hollow above the collar-bone).

The point of the triangular bandage will be loose and about level with the person's elbow, fold it round to the front and fasten it to the sling with a safety pin so that the fingernails are exposed. Check the circulation (page 38) – if necessary adjust the sling slightly.

Use your common sense

If you do not have a triangular bandage then support the limb in some other way.

You could for example:

- Fasten a person's jacket and slip the wrist above the fastening;
- Fold up the bottom edge of the jacket around the arm and use a safety pin to fix it in position;

- Pin the sleeve of the casualty's clothing so that the arm is supported;
- Use something like a belt, tie or pair of tights to support the limb.

Hand and fingers

These injuries are usually caused by a direct force and may be complicated by severe swelling and bleeding.

Symptoms and signs

- General symptoms and signs of a fracture (page 61).
- Person cannot use the fingers.
- Swelling and bruising at the site of the injury.

Treatment

Control any bleeding and treat wounds (page 36).

Protect the hand with a fold of soft padding.

Gently place the arm in an elevation sling and place a broad bandage (page 42) over the sling – tie it in front on the uninjured side with a reef knot (page 44).

Remove to hospital.

Pelvis

These fractures are usually the result of a person being crushed or by indirect force, for example, in car collisions. They may be complicated by internal injuries.

Symptoms and signs

- General symptoms and signs of a fracture (page 61).
- Pain and tenderness around the hips and groin – this is increased by movement.
- Casualty is unable to walk or stand although the legs do not seem injured.
- Person may want to pass water and this could be bloodstained.
- Symptoms and signs of shock (page 31).

Treatment

Place the casualty on the back with the legs straight (or if it is more comfortable place padding under the knees).

Place soft padding between the knees and ankles.

Apply a figure of eight bandage around the ankles and feet.

Fix another broad bandage around the knees tied on the uninjured side.

Treat for shock (page 31).

Remove to hospital.

Thigh and hip

A fractured thigh is a serious injury – it will probably cause heavy internal bleeding around the fracture and severe shock (page 31).

A broken hip-joint (involving the top of the thigh-bone) is often mistaken for a badly bruised hip – this is especially true after just a minor fall by an elderly person. If you are in any doubt – then treat as a fracture.

Symptoms and signs

- See symptoms and signs for fracture of leg. With the thigh and hip the leg might be shorter, the foot might be turned outwards.
- See symptoms and signs for shock (page 31).

Treatment

As for fractured leg.

Leg

There are two bones in the lower leg, places where fractures are likely to occur are shown in this drawing:

A fracture at the top of the shin bone could be caused by, for example, a car bumper hitting a person's leg.

A fracture at the bottom of the fibula could be caused by wrenching an ankle (and could be mistaken for a simple sprain – page 80).

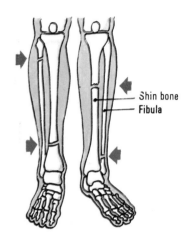

Shin bone
Fibula

Symptoms and signs

- General symptoms and signs of a fracture (page 61).
- The leg could be deformed.
- If both bones are broken, the foot and knee may not point in the same direction.
- There could be an open fracture (page 61).
- There could be symptoms and signs of shock (page 31).

Treatment

Lay the casualty down. Ask a helper to steady and support the injured leg by hand above and below the fracture site. Apply traction at the ankle. If the arrival of the ambulance is imminent, maintain traction and support until it arrives. Treat to minimise shock.

Otherwise place broad bandages (page 42) under the feet and knees but do not tie them yet.

Gently put plenty of soft padding between the knees and ankles.

Very gently move the good leg alongside the injured one.

Tie a figure of eight bandage around the feet and ankles and a broad bandage around the knees. Tie the knots on the uninjured side.

If splints are available. For a fractured leg, place a padded splint between the legs and bandage as for a rough journey.

If the thigh is fractured place an additional long splint and padding alongside the fractured limb from the armpit to the foot.

Place extra padding where the splint might become uncomfortable (at the ankles and hips for example) and in any hollows.

If casualty is to be transported by first aiders:

Use more padding and additional bandages.

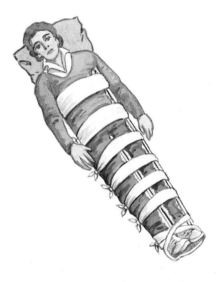

Place two extra bandages above and below the fractured site. Tie off on the uninjured side.

You need three more broad bandages – one around the chest (just below the armpits) and the other round the pelvis level with the hips. Then bandage the lower legs and splints as for a rough journey.

Tie knots on the uninjured side.

Treat for shock (page 31).

When the legs are securely fixed, raise them slightly (be very gentle).

Remove to hospital.

Foot

These fractures can be caused by direct injuries or by twisting, for example, in a fall or jump.

Symptoms and signs

- General symptoms and signs of a fracture (page 61).
- Pain and tenderness which is increased by movement.
- Tenderness at the site of the injury.
- Person cannot move the foot properly.
- Swelling, bruising and deformity can occur.

Treatment

Lay the casualty down.

Support the foot and gently remove footwear.

Raise and support foot on a folded blanket and dress any wounds if present.

Arrange removal to hospital keeping the foot raised and supported.

Injuries to Muscles, Ligaments and Joints

Joints • Sprains • Dislocation • Knee Injuries • Muscles • Cramp • Strain • Hernia

JOINTS

Joints are formed by the linking of bones and may be immovable or movable. **Immovable** joints in the body are, for example, between the bones forming the skull.

The three types of **movable** joints are:

Ball and socket joints – formed by the rounded head of one bone fitting into the cup-shaped cavity of another – these allow free movement in all directions, for example, the hip or shoulder.

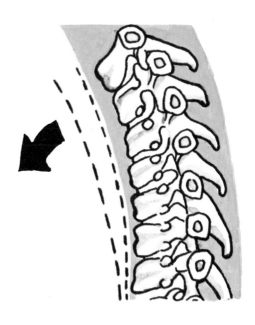

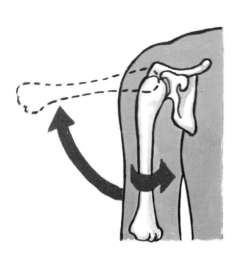

Slightly movable joints – found where only a small amount of movement is needed – for example the spine or the foot.

Hinged joints – these let bones move in one direction to bend or straighten. Examples include the elbow or knee.

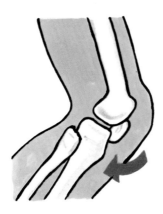

Inside the knee joint are two pieces of cartilage; if the knee is suddenly wrenched (for example, in a game of football) these cartilages may be torn (page 81).

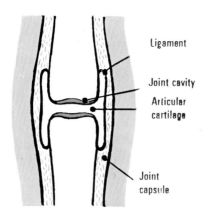

Ligament

Joint cavity

Articular cartilage

Joint capsule

The knee is not the only joint containing cartilages, in fact the ends of bones in every movable joint are covered with cartilage. The joint is lubricated by fluid produced from the lining of the bag (capsule) enclosing the joint. The whole joint is strengthened by strong bands of tissue called ligaments.

SPRAIN

This is when the ligaments and tissues at a joint are wrenched or torn.

Symptoms and signs

- Pain and tenderness at the joint which increase with movement.
- Swelling (and later bruising).

Treatment (RICE)

Rest and support the joint in the most comfortable position.

Carefully uncover the joint and if the sprain is recent, apply an ice bag or a cold compress for 30 minutes (page 117) or a firm bandage over a good layer of cotton wool.

Elevate the injured limb.

If symptoms persist, seek medical aid.

Some symptoms and signs are similar to those for fractures – if in doubt, treat as a fracture.

DISLOCATION

This type of injury is the displacement of one or more bones at a joint. It usually occurs in the shoulder, elbow, thumb, finger or lower jaw.

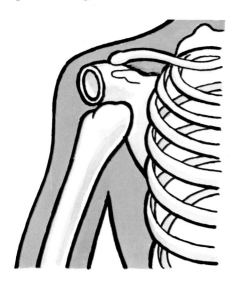

A fracture may also have occurred – if in doubt treat as a fracture (page 72).

Remove to hospital.

Symptoms and signs

- Severe and often sickening pain at or near the joint.
- The casualty cannot move the part.
- The joint is misshapen.
- Swelling (and later bruising).

Treatment

Do not attempt to move the bones to their normal position.

Support and secure the injured part in the most comfortable position using pillows or cushions. Immobilise with bandages and slings if available.

KNEE INJURIES

Symptoms and signs

Severe pain is felt.

The knee may be bent and can possibly be bent more or be locked.

The knee should not be straightened – attempts to do so may cause pain.

Swelling may occur because of fluid collecting in the joint.

Treatment

Do not alter the bent position of the knee.

Support the leg in the most comfortable position for the casualty.

Protect the knee by placing soft padding around the joint – apply a bandage (but not so tight as to cause discomfort or affect circulation) (page 38).

Support the knee by placing a small pillow, folded blanket or coat underneath it.

Give nothing by mouth.

Remove to hospital.

MUSCLES

These produce movement by tightening and relaxing.

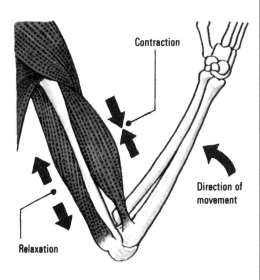

Contraction

Direction of movement

Relaxation

There are two types:

Involuntary muscles are found in the heart and blood vessels, the intestines, stomach and most of the internal organs. They continue their work at all times, even when we sleep, and most are not under the control of the will.

Voluntary muscles help in movements when we wish them to. They may be attached to bones and produce bending or straightening of joints.

CRAMP

This is the sudden involuntary and painful shortening of a muscle or group of muscles.

Cramp may be caused by poor co-ordination during exercise, chilling fo example when swimming, or by excessive loss of salt and body fluids due to sweating, diarrhoea, etc.

Symptoms and signs

- Pain.
- Tightness (or "spasm") in the affected muscle.
- Casualty is unable to relax the tight muscles.

Treatment
In the hand

Gently but firmly straighten the finger and massage the area.

In the thigh

Straighten the knee and raise the leg with one hand under the heel. Use the other hand to press down the knee. Massage the area gently.

In the calf

Straighten the knee and draw the foot towards the shin. Massage the area gently.

In the foot

Straighten the toes and get the casualty to stand on the ball of the foot. Massage the area gently.

STRAIN

This is the over-stretching and possibly tearing of muscle or groups of muscles.

Symptoms and signs

- Sudden sharp pain at the site of the injury.
- The pain spreads outwards, giving stiffness and/or cramp.
- Swelling.

Treatment (RICE)

Rest in the most comfortable position.

If the strain is recent, apply an ice bag or a cold compress (page 117) for at least 30 minutes.

Compress the injured part with a thick layer of cotton wool and a bandage.

Elevate the limb.

If in doubt, treat as a fracture.

Arrange for medical aid.

HERNIA (*Rupture*)

This is the protrusion of some of the abdominal contents through the abdomen's muscular wall under the skin. There is a swelling which comes on after excercise, lifting or coughing. It occurs most frequently in the groin, navel, or through the scar of an abdominal operation.

A "strangulated hernia", when a piece of the bowel is nipped, is an urgent surgical problem.

Symptoms and signs

- Painless swelling which may persist or worsen.
- Sudden painful swelling with possible nausea and vomiting. This is a strangulated hernia.

Treatment

Do not attempt to reduce the swelling.

Reassure the casualty.

If vomiting occurs or seems likely, place in the recovery position (page 19).

Otherwise lay the casualty down and support the head and shoulders, bend and support the knees.

Seek medical aid.

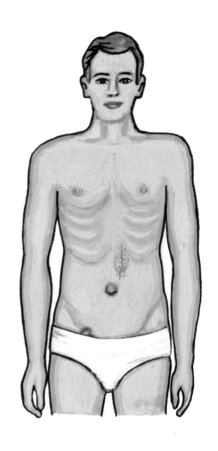

Aches, Foreign Bodies, Poisoning

Aches ● *Headache* ● *Neckache* ● *Backache* ● *Abdominal Pain* ● *Toothache* ● *Foreign Bodies* ● *Stings* ● *Poisons*

ACHES

An ache is a continuous dull pain and may be a symptom of another condition or injury which need not be sited exactly where the ache is (referred pain). If you cannot diagnose the problem you should try to help reduce the pain.

Remember

You **must not** give a casualty **any** type of medicine. (The person might, however, have medicine and choose to take it.)

An ache might be a symptom of a more severe injury or illness.

HEADACHE

This could be due to an injury to the neck or spine (pages 54 and 55).

Common causes are: common cold, stress, eye-strain, pressure or lack of sleep or food.

Treatment

Place a cold compress or a covered hot-water bottle on the person's forehead.

If possible advise the person to lie down in a darkened room.

If the headache carries on for long or if the person has other symptoms (such as feeling of nausea, vomiting, fever, stiff neck, disturbed vision, signs of a head injury, confusion or gradual loss of consciousness (page 52), **seek medical help.** See also pages 64 to 66.

NECKACHE

This could be caused by a "whiplash" injury (page 66). Common causes are: sitting or lying in one position for too long, exposure to draughts or nervous tension.

Treatment

Hold a covered hot-water bottle or heated pad against the area and get the person to move the neck gently.

If the person has other symptoms (such as swelling, nausea, vomiting, headache, confusion, loss of consciousness or signs of injury) then seek medical help (page 67).

BACKACHE

This can be a symptom of many different problems, for example, a strain (page 83), poor posture or displaced disc in the spine. Backache may also be caused by disorder elsewhere in the body, for example, kidney infection.

Treatment

If there is a strain then treat as shown on page 83. Otherwise, place a covered hot water bottle on the area.

If the symptoms carry on for long, if the temperature is high, if the person cannot move the legs or the legs are weak or there is a loss (or abnormal) sensation or if there are problems with the bladder or bowel then seek medical help at once.

ABDOMINAL PAIN

There are many causes of abdominal pain – generally it is not serious if it lasts less than half an hour and there are no other symptoms and signs.

Treatment

To relieve pain, place the person in the most comfortable position, usually half sitting, with the head and shoulders supported and knees bent.

If vomiting is likely, place in the recovery position (page 19).

Keep the casualty lying down and comfortable.

Treat for shock if necessary (page 31).

If the pain lasts for more than half an hour or you have any doubts about the person's condition – seek medical help.

TOOTHACHE

Treatment

Dab the crown of the tooth, not the gum, with oil of cloves (if available).

Rinse the mouth with hot or cold water as preferred.

Advise the person to see a doctor or dentist without delay.

FOREIGN BODIES

A "foreign body" is anything which should not enter the body but which does. It can go through a wound (penetrating) or one of the body's own openings (swallowed or inserted).

Action and treatment

Loose foreign bodies (such as grit) can be washed out or gently removed with a clean swab or tweezers. The wound should then be dressed (page 40).

Embedded foreign bodies must be removed at a hospital. Treat as on page 38 and seek medical help.

If the casualty is actually fixed (for example on railings) then the fire brigade will be needed. You should not try to lift them off.

Swallowed foreign objects mean that you need medical help. (See also poisoning on page 89).

Foreign bodies in the eye

Particles of dust or grit or loose lashes, insects or small fragments of metal or glass may lodge in the eyeball or under the eyelid causing considerable discomfort and inflammation if not quickly removed.

If the foreign body is:

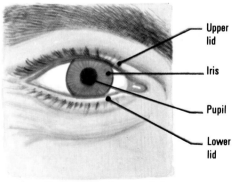

Upper lid

Iris

Pupil

Lower lid

– on the coloured part of the eye
– embedded in the eye or
– stuck to the eye

then **do not** try to remove it, treat as follows:

Treatment

Tell the casualty not to move the eye.

Cover it with an eye pad (if necessary prevent eye movement by putting eye pads on both eyes.

Remove to hospital.

See also "chemicals in the eye" (page 98).

A bit of dust or an eyelash can cause great discomfort and normally can be removed quite easily.

Symptoms and signs

- Casualty's eye is painful and itches.
- Casualty's vision may be impaired.
- Watering of affected eye.
- Casualty's eye is red.

Treatment

Tell the person **not** to rub the eye.

Ask to sit facing the light and lean back.

Stand behind and hold the chin steady with one hand.

Use the thumb and forefinger of the other hand to separate the eyelids.

Ask the person to look right, left, up and down (this will let you see every part of the eye).

If you can see the foreign body then try to wash it out using:

Sterile water solution and an eye irrigator or (if these are not available) tap water and a jug or running tap water.

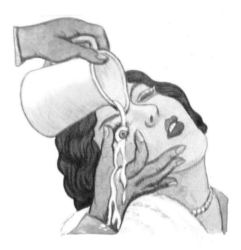

Tilt the head towards the injured side (so that the water drips off the face, away from the uninjured eye).

If the foreign body does not wash away or if no water is available (and the foreign body is not embedded or stuck to the eye) then lift it off with a moist swab or the damp corner of a clean handkerchief.

If the foreign body is under the upper lid then ask the person to look down. Take hold of the eyelashes and pull the upper lid downwards and out, over the lower lid. The lower eyelashes will probably brush the object off.

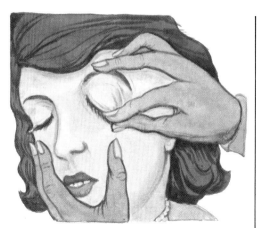

If the foreign body does not come off the upper lid then get the person to blink the eye under water in the hope that the foreign body will float off.

If you cannot remove the foreign body then cover the eye with an eye pad or gauze wrapped round a piece of cotton wool. Bandage lightly.

Seek medical help.

Foreign body in the ear

These are most common in young children.

Symptoms and signs

- Pain.
- Hearing affected.
- Possible noise from, for example, an insect.

Treatment

Reassure the casualty.

Do not try to remove a foreign body.

If it is an insect then tilt the person's head so that you can pour water into the ear, then flood the ear with tepid water.

Seek medical aid or remove to hospital.

Foreign body in the nose

This is most common in very young children.

Symptoms and signs

- Casualty has difficulty in breathing through the nose.
- Nose might appear swollen.
- Discharge (often blood-stained) appearing from one or both sides of the nose.

Treatment

Do not try to remove the object.

Keep the person quiet and advise to breathe through the mouth.

Seek medical help or remove to hospital.

Swallowed foreign body

Children in particular often swallow small objects.

Treatment

Calm the person, and reassure the parents if the casualty is a child.

Seek medical help or remove to hospital.

Do not give anything to eat or drink.

STINGS

Insects and jellyfish cause stings which are more painful and alarming than they are dangerous.

Symptoms and signs

- Unexpected sharp pain.
- Swelling around the area with a central reddened puncture point.
- Some people who are allergic may have severe shock (page 31) or difficulty in breathing (Chapter 2).

Treatment

If an insect's sting is present then remove it using tweezers, holding them as near to the skin as possible.

To relieve pain and swelling, apply a cold compress (page 117); surgical spirit or a solution of bicarbonate of soda.

If pain and swelling persist or increase over the next day or so, advise the person to seek medical help.

If the sting is in the mouth, give ice to suck or rinse the mouth with cold water or a mouthwash of one teaspoonful of bicarbonate of soda to a glass of water.

If breathing becomes difficult then place in the recovery position (page 19).

Remove to hospital.

POISONS

A poison is any substance which if taken into the body in sufficient quantity can cause temporary or permanent damage.

Poisons enter the body (either accidentally or deliberately):

Through the mouth

- Eating or drinking poisonous substances.

Through the lungs

- Breathing in industrial gases, fumes from heaters, car exhaust fumes, smoke from some burning furniture, "glue-sniffing".

Through the skin

- By being bitten by some animals, insects or snakes;
- By injection;
- By "soaking through" the skin (absorption) – for example through contact with some garden chemicals.

Poisons work in different ways – either stopping respiration, heartbeat, irritating the food passages or burning the parts of the body which they touch.

General symptoms and signs

These will be different for each poison and method of entry into the body – try to get an accurate **history** of the incident from the casualty or onlookers.

- Look for any containers or other clues which are close by.
- Casualty may be delirious and have convulsions (without a history of any illness).
- Symptoms and signs of asphyxia (page 13).
- Person may lose consciousness (page 52).
- If the poison was swallowed the person may vomit or suffer from diarrhoea.
- There could be burns around the mouth.

General treatment

Quickly ask a conscious casualty what has happened (the person may lose consciousness at any time).

Do not try to make the casualty vomit – it will not help and may make things worse.

If the lips appear to be burning, cool them by giving a **conscious** person water or milk to drink.

Even if the casualty is conscious and breathing normally, place in the recovery position (page 19), he may vomit.

If breathing and heartbeat stop apply artificial ventilation and chest compression (pages 15 and 17).

Use your common sense

Take care not to contaminate yourself with any poison that may be around the casualty's mouth.

Remove to hospital immediately (send any samples of vomit or empty containers with the casualty).

Poisons in the house

Young children are especially at risk in a house:

- From medicines and tablets;
- From cleaning materials;
- From chemicals we use, and
- Even from things like make-up.

Symptoms and signs

- As on page 89 (particularly vomiting and abdominal pain).

Treatment

As on page 89 and remove to hospital immediately.

Use your common sense

If you see something that could be dangerous – tell someone or remove the danger before a child is poisoned.

Always make sure that all bottles and jars holding poisonous substances are kept out of the reach of children.

Keep all medicines out of the reach of children (even containers with "child resistant lids" can be opened eventually).

Never keep poisonous substances in, for example, lemonade bottles.

Food poisoning

This is caused by germs getting into food which is not stored or cooked properly.

Symptoms and signs

Not all of these may appear immediately.
- Casualty feels nauseated and may vomit.
- Person may have abdominal pain.
- The person may have a headache.
- The person may develop diarrhoea.
- The person may have a fever.
- The casualty may have symptoms and signs of shock (page 31).

Treatment

Get the person to rest.

Give plenty of drinks.

Seek medical help (possibly remove to hospital).

Poisonous plants

Certain common plants are dangerous if eaten or, in some cases, if touched.

Laburnum, deadly nightshade and death cap fungus are examples – they cause symptoms and signs similar to **food poisoning.**

Treatment

Keep the airway open (page 14).

Remove to hospital immediately.

Burns and Extremes of Temperature

Burns • Dry Burns and Scalds • Mouth and Throat • Chemical • Electrical • Sunburn •
Heat Exhaustion • Hypothermia • Frostbite

BURNS AND SCALDS

These are injuries to the body tissues
caused by heat, chemicals or radiation.
Most burns will need medical attention.

Types of burns
DRY BURNS
The result of contact with flames, hot
electrical equipment, or a fast moving
object.

SCALDS
The result of contact with wet heat such
as steam, hot water or fat.

Cold burns
- The result of contact with something
  very cold.

Chemical burns
- The result of contact with chemicals
  (including things found in the house
  (see poisoning, page 90).

Electrical burns
- Caused by electrical currents (page 26)
  or lightning.

Radiaton burns
- Caused by rays usually from the sun
  and light reflected from bright surfaces.

Classification of burns
The size of the burn will help you to
decide:

- Whether the person should see a
  doctor or go to hospital;
- Whether the person is likely to have
  shock (page 31).
- What treatment to give.

The two key things are the **area** and
the **depth** of the burn.

Area
Any non-superficial burn larger than the
size of a hand, or which is the result of
electrical contact must be seen by a doctor
or receive hospital treatment.

Use your common sense

A burn which covers half the arm
would obviously need hospital treatment.

Depth

Symptoms and Signs

A **superficial** burn only goes into the outer layers of the skin.

- Redness, swelling and extreme tenderness.

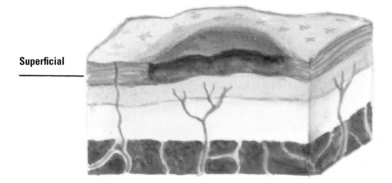

Superficial

A **partial thickness** burn goes a little deeper.

- Blisters, swelling and very red appearance around the burn. (These burns may become infected so you need medical help.)

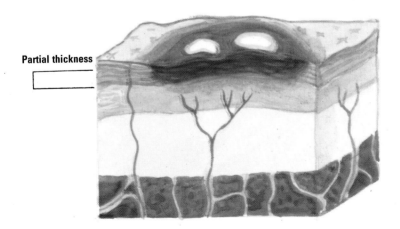

Partial thickness

A **full thickness** burn involves all layers of the skin.

- Skin may be pale, waxy or even charred.
- There will be **little** pain (because the nerves have been damaged).
- **Full thickness burns always need medical attention.**

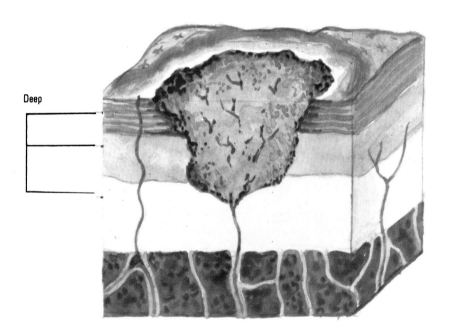

Deep

DRY BURNS AND SCALDS

These are the most common types of burn – without prompt help the person could be severely burnt, causing shock and possible death.

Symptoms and signs of shock (page 31) will depend on the **severity and area** of the burn.

Action and treatment

If clothing is on fire then lay the casualty down and put out the flames either with water or:

- If your own clothes catch fire and no help is available then wrap yourself tightly in something and lie down.

- If the accident happens indoors, **do not** let the casualty panic and rush outside (this would make the flames worse).

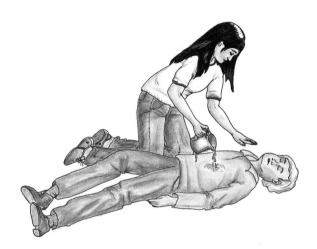

- Lay the person flat on the ground – **do not** roll them along the ground.

- Wrap the person tightly in a coat, curtain, non-cellular blanket, rug or other heavy material that will not catch fire.

The most important thing to remember when treating burns and scalds is that they must be cooled as quickly as possible. The best way to do that is gently to flood the area with cold water.

Carefully remove any clothing which has been soaked in boiling fluid (for example, hot coffee or tea).

Cooled, dry burnt clothing should **not** be removed.

If you are in any doubt about how serious the burn is, then seek medical help.

Treatment for minor burns and scalds

Reassure the person

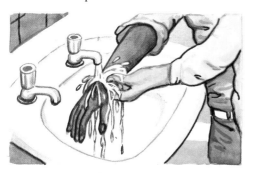

Place the injured part under slowly running cold water or immerse it in cold water for at least 10 minutes (longer if the pain persists).

Use your common sense

If there is no water then use any harmless fluid – milk, lemonade or whatever is available.

Gently remove any rings, watches, belts, shoes or other tight clothing from the injured area before area starts to swell.

Cover the burn with a clean (preferably sterile) non-fluffy dressing (page 40), or a clean polythene bag or kitchen film as a temporary dressing.

Do not use adhesive dressings ("plasters").

Do not put any creams, fats or lotions on the area.

Do not break blisters, remove loose skin or interfere with the injury in any way.

If in any doubt, seek medical help.

Treatment for severe burns and scalds

Check airway (page 14), breathing and circulation (page 19).

Lay the person down and make as comfortable as possible. Try to stop the burn touching the ground.

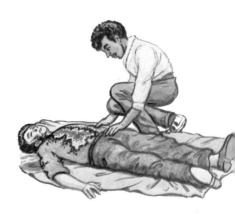

Gently remove any rings, watches, belts or tight clothing before swelling starts.

Do not remove from the injured area anything that is sticking to a burn but otherwise remove any clothing that has been soaked in boiling fluid (use your common sense, do not get scalded yourself).

Gently flood the area with cold water.

Cover the injury with a sterile, unmedicated dressing (page 40) (or similar non-fluffy material or a clean polythene bag or kitchen film) and fix in place with a bandage (page 42).

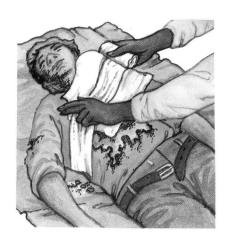

Do not apply any creams, fats, lotions or ointments to the burn.

Do not break any blisters, remove any loose skin or interfere with the injury in any way.

Immobilise a badly burned limb (see fractures, Chapter 6).

Treat for shock (page 31).

If the casualty is conscious then give them sips of cold water at frequent intervals.

If breathing and heartbeat stop then apply artificial ventilation and chest compression (pages 15 and 17).

If the casualty is unconscious but breathing normally, place in the recovery position (page 19).

Remove to hospital.

BURNS IN THE MOUTH AND THROAT

There is a great danger of asphyxia with these injuries as the swelling caused by the burn might block the airway (page 13).

They are usually caused by drinking very hot liquids, swallowing chemicals (page 90) or breathing-in very hot air (a person who has escaped from a fire might have done this).

Symptoms and signs

- Severe pain.
- Damaged skin around the mouth.
- Difficulty in breathing.
- Possible unconsciousness (page 51).
- Symptoms and signs of shock (page 31).

Treatment

Reassure the person.

For a minor scald give sips of cold water at frequent intervals.

Remove any tight clothing or jewellery from around the neck and chest.

If breathing and heartbeat stop then apply artificial ventilation and chest compression (pages 15 and 17).

If the casualty is unconscious but breathing normally then place in the recovery position (page 19).

Treat for shock (page 31).

Remove to hospital immediately.

CHEMICAL BURNS

Many strong chemicals are used and stored – not only in factories but even in houses (cleaning materials like bleach or liquids used for removing paint for example). See page 89 where the danger of chemicals as poisons is described.

Burns from chemicals on the skin need urgent treatment.

> ## Use your common sense:
> **Do not turn yourself into another casualty by burning your skin.**

Symptoms and signs

- The casualty's skin may be stinging.
- The skin may look stained or be red.
- Blistering and peeling may develop.

Treatment

Flood the area with slowly running cold water for 10 to 20 minutes (the used water will have the chemical in it so make sure that it drains away safely).

> ## Use your common sense

Do not get the chemical on **your** skin.

Gently and carefully remove any clothing which has got chemical on it; still keep the water running over the injury while you are doing this.

Continue the treatment for severe burns (page 96).

Remove to hospital immediately.

Chemical burns in the eye

If the surface of the eye is damaged then severe scarring and even blindness can occur.

Symptoms and signs

- Intense pain.
- The damaged eye cannot tolerate light.
- The eye may be tightly closed.
- The eye may be red, swollen or watering. (The casualty may want to rub the eye.)

Treatment

Do not let the person rub the eye.

Hold the person's face under gently running cold water so that the water washes the eye and then drips off the face (**not** into the other eye); or

get the person to put that side of their face in a bowl of cold water and blink; or

sit or lay the person down with the head back tilted towards the injured side. Protect the uninjured side, gently open the eyelid and pour sterile water from an eye irrigator (or a glass of tap water) over it.

Check that both surfaces of the eyelids have been well washed – you may need to pull the eyelids open (be firm but gentle).

Lightly dress the eye with a sterile eye pad or a piece of clean, non-fluffy material.

Remove to hospital immediately.

ELECTRICAL BURNS

A burn may occur when electricity passes through the body – the burn might seem small on the surface but is probably very deep and damage to the body tissues below may be very severe. Other dangers from electricity include asphyxia (page 13) and broken bones (page 60).

Symptoms and signs

- Redness, swelling, scorching or charring at the place where the electricity entered the body and where it left.
- Possible unconsciousness.
- Symptoms and signs of asphyxia are possible (page 13) (breathing and heartbeat may have stopped).
- Symptoms and signs of shock (page 31).

Action and treatment

Remove from the source as described on page 24.

Use your common sense:
Do not turn yourself into another casualty

Treat as for a severe burn (page 96).

Remove to hospital immediately.

Effects of extremes of temperature

The body works properly if the temperature stays between 36 and 37°C (97 to 99°F), hot weather can cause **sunburn or heat exhaustion**. On the other hand, if the body gets **too cold** then other injuries may occur, they are **hypothermia** and **frostbite**.

SUNBURN

The sun can cause severe burns – swimmers or people who feel safe because of a cool wind are often victims.

Symptoms and signs

- Casualty's skin is hot, red, tender and swollen with possible blistering.

Treatment

Remove the person to the shade and cool the skin by sponging with cold water – be gentle.

Give the person sips of cold water at frequent intervals.

If there are blisters, **do not** break them and seek medical help immediately.

HEAT EXHAUSTION

This is a problem that can affect people in hot weather. It is caused because the casualty loses too much water and salt by sweating.

It is even more likely to occur if the person has an upset stomach with diarrhoea and vomiting.

Symptoms and signs

- The casualty may feel exhausted but restless.
- The person may have a headache and feel tired, dizzy and nauseated.
- There could be cramp in the legs and abdomen caused by lack of salt, (page 82).

- The person's face will be pale, the skin will feel cold and clammy.
- Breathing becomes rapid and shallow.
- The pulse is rapid and weak.
- Temperature remains normal or falls.
- The casualty may faint on movement.

Treatment

Lay the person down in a cool place.

If conscious give sips of cold water to drink – if the person is sweating a lot, has cramp, diarrhoea and/or is vomiting then add half a teaspoonful of salt to each $\frac{1}{2}$ litre (1 pint) of water.

If the casualty becomes unconscious but is breathing normally then place in the recovery position (page 19).

Seek medical help.

HYPOTHERMIA

This is commonly caused by someone:

- Being in cold water (for example a person falling in the sea);
- Not having proper shelter (for example a climber stuck on a hill side);
- Simply being in a cold house for a long time.

Some people are more at risk from hypothermia, they include:

- Older people (particularly those who live alone and who might be worried about spending money on heating);
- People with medical conditions such as diabetes;
- People who are affected by drugs or alcohol;
- Infants, particularly newborn babies.

Symptoms and signs

- The person passes through several stages of discomfort and disability – death may occur rapidly (especially in the case of people who are, for example, in the sea, or in cold, wet and exposed conditions on land).

The different stages of hypothermia are:

- Person feels miserably cold.
- The skin is pale (except with infants – page 102).
- The casualty feels cold to the touch.
- The casualty might shiver uncontrollably.
- The shivering stops and the person does not move or talk properly.
- The casualty does not understand what is happening and may behave unreasonably (page 52).
- The pulse and breathing rate slow down.
- Unconsciousness, breathing and pulse become difficult to detect.

This last stage might make you think the person is dead when they are not. Never presume that the casualty is dead simply because you cannot detect breathing or a pulse.

Treatment

If casualty is at home or in shelter:
Remove the casualty's outer clothing, and replace any wet clothing with dry.

Place her in a bed which has been previously warmed.

If she can climb into the bath unaided, and is not elderly. place her in a hot bath, at a temperature which is bearable when tested with your elbow (approximately 40°C/104°F). Test the water at intervals, and replenish if necessary. When the casualty's skin colour returns to normal and her pulse rate improves, return her to a warm bed.

Give her hot drinks and high energy food, e.g., chocolate.

If casualty is in the open:
Carry the casualty to a warm shelter as quickly and as gently as possible. Insulate the ground she is to lie on, e.g., with dry bracken.

Place her in a sleeping bag or cover her with blankets, newspaper, silver foil, or other insulating materials.

Whilst awaiting rescue, lie beside the casualty so that you share your body heat with her.

Send for help (ideally, you should send two people).

When help arrives, evacuate the casualty by stretcher to hospital or to a house to await the ambulance or helicopter.

If she is conscious, give her hot drinks and high energy food.

If she is unconscious, open her airway and check breathing. Complete the ABC of Resuscitation if necessary, and place her in the recovery position (page 19).

Hypothermia in infants

Babies have difficulty controlling their body temperatures. A danger is that they may **look** very healthy (pink skin), but may be suffering from hypothermia.

Symptoms and signs

- The baby is unusually quiet, drowsy and limp.
- The baby will refuse food.
- The face, hands and feet may be bright pink and healthy looking.

Treatment

As with adults.

FROSTBITE

This occurs when the extremities of the body such as the ears, nose, chin, hands and feet get **very** cold. It might just freeze the skin (superficial) or it could freeze the skin and other body tissues (deep).

If frostbite **and** hypothermia are present then **treat hypothermia first.**

Symptoms and signs

- The casualty feels prickling pain in the area, followed by a gradual numbness.
- The person might not be able to move the part normally.
- The skin feels hard and stiff.
- The skin looks waxy-white or mottled blue in colour.

Treatment

Remove to shelter and **gently** take off any clothing from the area.

Remove any tight items (such as rings, watches, gloves or boots).

Warm the area by using some warm part of the casualty or yourself.

For example:
Hands could be placed in the armpits. You could warm the feet in your armpits. Cover ears, nose or face with warm hands.

Do not rub the injury or put any ointments on the area.

Carry on until colour and sensation return.

Place the injured part in water that is hot but not unbearable when you place your elbow in it.

Do not use any form of heater to warm the injury. (It must thaw gradually).

Do not let the casualty walk on a "defrosted" foot.

Do not attempt to thaw out a joint if the casualty will later be exposed to cold on a journey, as to freeze – thaw – refreeze is disastrous to tissues. Simply cover the affected part in dry gauze or wool and loose bandaging or enclose it in a plastic bag.

If re-warming reverses the signs within an hour, stop treatment but do not re-expose to cold.

Do not break any blisters or apply ointments, etc. to the area.

Raise the injured limb.

Lightly cover the parts with soft dressings.

Remove to hospital.

Lifting and Carrying

At an incident you should never move a severely injured or ill person unless:

● There is immediate danger to life
● Medical help is not readily available.

You are responsible for the safety of the casualty and so you must **always** make sure that the condition will not be made worse by handling or movement, for example, large wounds and fractures must be immobilised (page 62).

If the person is to be moved then as far as possible, the casualty should be kept in the treatment position. The person must be watched to check that the condition does not get worse. The aim is to get the casualty to the destination without making worse or causing discomfort.

If the person is being taken to a hospital then you should normally arrange for an ambulance.

Remember that you should try not to move the casualty while help is coming. First Aid treatment should be given on the spot. The only exception to this rule is if the casualty's life is in danger (from fire, for example) or if your life would be in danger if you did not move, for example on a motorway.

If you do have to move the person:
● Then do so as quickly as possible without putting yourself in danger;
● Never try to move a seriously injured casualty on your own if help is available;
● Always make sure that your helpers (and the casualty) understand what is happening and
● Take charge – give simple instructions at each stage (for example, "lift **now**").

LIFTING

Lifting is a skill and you must do it correctly in order not to injure yourself or hurt the casualty. If you do have to let go, let the person slide to the ground causing as little damage to the injury as possible. **Do not** injure your back by trying to stop the casualty falling.

The method you use to carry or lift the person will depend upon:
● What type of injury the person has;
● How severe the injuries are;
● How many helpers you have;
● What equipment or other facilities are available;
● The size of the casualty;
● How far you have to carry the person; and
● The route (for example, is the ground rough?)

Guidelines

Whatever method you decide on, there are guidelines which you should follow:

- **Do not** try to lift too heavy a weight by yourself (use bystanders to help).

- Use the most powerful muscles of your body (the thigh, hip and shoulder).
- Keep the weight as close to your body as possible.
- Bend your knees, not your back.
- Place your feet comfortably apart (so that you are well balanced).

METHODS OF CARRYING BY ONE FIRST AIDER

If help is available, **do not** try to move a casualty on your own.

Drag

This should **only be** used if the casualty is unable to stand and has to be moved quickly from danger and cannot be lifted.

Fold the person's arms across the chest.

If the person is wearing a jacket or coat, unbutton it and pull it back up under the person's head. Crouch behind and pull along.

If the person is **not** wearing a jacket then place your arms under the shoulders, grasp the armpits and pull (cradle the casualty's head on your forearms).

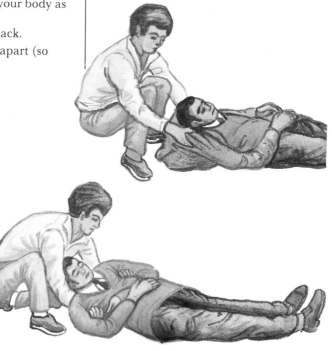

Cradle

To carry small children or other people who do not weigh much.

Simply pass one arm around the person's body above the waist and the other under the thighs and lift.

Pick-a-back

If the person is small, light, conscious and able to hold on to you then use this method of carrying.

Human crutch

This should **not** be used if an arm is injured and is only suitable if the person can walk with your help.

Stand at the person's injured side. Place the casualty's arm around your neck and hold the hand.

Put your other arm around the person's waist and hold the clothes at the hip.

METHODS OF CARRYING BY TWO FIRST AIDERS

Two-handed seat

Squat facing each other on either side of the casualty.

Each of you should pass one arm round the casualty just below the shoulders. Grasp the casualty's clothing.

Raise the person's legs slightly, pass your other arms under the middle of the thigh and grasp each other's wrists.

Stand up together, step off with the outside leg and walk with ordinary paces.

PLACING A BLANKET UNDER A CASUALTY

With all injuries it is likely that the casualty will suffer from shock (page 31), this will be made worse by losing body heat. With a casualty who is lying down, more heat will be lost into the ground than into the air. Therefore if you have only one blanket it will be more useful **under** than over the person.

Use your common sense

If placing a blanket under a casualty might worsen the injuries then **do not** disturb – place the blanket **over** the person.

Action

You will need at least three people to help you, they should follow your instructions.

First of all, make certain that the blanket will hold the weight of the casualty, if necessary.

To test the blanket:

Lay it on the ground;
Get one person to lie on it while two others try to lift it.

To get the blanket in position:

Roll it lengthwise for half its width;
Place the roll against the injured side of the casualty (or the most severely injured if both are hurt).

Now the team should work together gently and slowly turning the casualty on the side away from the blanket (injured side up). The roll of blanket should be moved up against the person's back. The casualty should now be gently turned back over the roll of blanket (far enough over to let it be unrolled). Turn the casualty into the treatment position again.

See page 107.

STRETCHERS

A stretcher is used to minimise the risk of further injury when carrying a seriously ill or injured casualty to an ambulance or shelter.

Of the stretchers in general use the most common are: the "standard" or Furley stretcher, the "Utila" or lightweight version in metal of the "standard". A fully adjustable light metal stretcher bed on wheels ("trolley") is carried in most ambulances.

You might have to help move casualties, loading stretchers and showing onlookers how to help. Remember to keep the casualty level and supported.

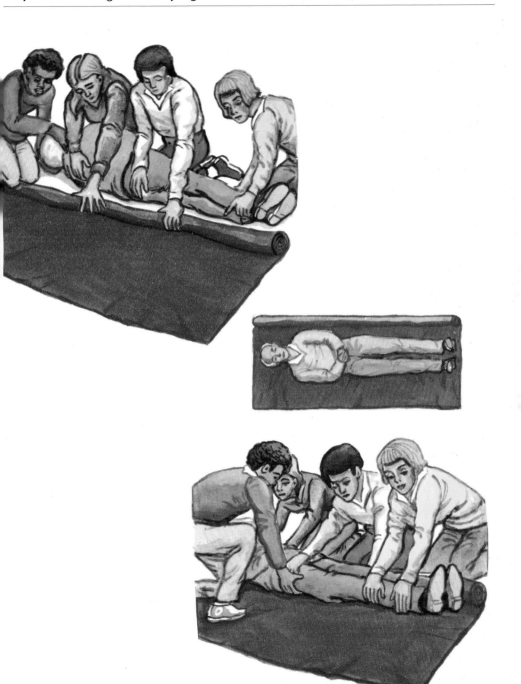

First Aid in Action

> *In this chapter you will see how some of the techniques which are described in this book might be used at just one incident, a serious road accident.*

Let us imagine the story behind this picture:

It is raining and so you are hurrying to get home.

You hear the sound of a crash and run towards the noise, when you arrive you see that a motorcyclist is lying on the ground, not moving. You can also see that a car has crashed into a tree. The driver of the car is slumped over the steering wheel and you can hear the lady in the passenger seat who is crying and shouting for help.

You are probably nervous (and even scared) because of what you see.

So, what should you do? – Over the next few pages we will go through the steps which a First Aider would take.

STEP 1 – Assess the situation

Appear calm and take charge, for example the woman in the car will not know that you are a First Aider until you tell her. She will just expect you immediately to run for help – whereas you might need to carry out urgent treatment to save someone's life.

Ensure safety, of yourself as well as the casualty. One or two more people might have arrived at the scene of the accident by now – you should ask them to help you by stopping the traffic.

To remove the risk of fire, your helpers should:

Switch off car engines (in case of petrol leaks).

Stop smoking.

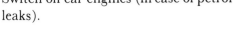

Look for warning signs (especially if a lorry or tanker is involved).

To help you, they should:

Get help by dialling 999.

Warn other people:

Do what you say. For example you might need to tell them **not** to pull that driver out of the car or move the motorcyclist.

The motorcyclist could be run over by another car – or you could be hit as you examine him, so bystanders could use warning lights or hazard signs.

Another danger might be the way that the car is leaning by the tree, the handbrake will not be on and so it might move, trapping you or worsening the driver's injuries. Someone should put blocks by its wheels to stop it moving.

So, in just a few moments you have assessed the situation and are using bystanders to make certain that the situation does not get worse.

STEP 2 – Diagnosis

While the other people are doing all these things, you must be starting your diagnosis, particularly to see if anyone needs urgent treatment.

You have many questions that need answering, for example:

Who is injured?
The motorcyclist, the driver of the car and the passenger all seem to be.

How many casualties are there?
Is it just those three or was there anyone else? – sometimes casualties stumble away from an accident, or someone may have been thrown from the car.

Are there any children hidden?
Is anyone lying by the back seat of the car?

Is anyone unconscious?
The motorcyclist seems to be and perhaps the driver of the car is. They may have fractured their spines.

You can get the answers to those questions by quickly looking round and by calmly talking to anyone who is conscious, for example that woman passenger. Remember that any casualty will be very frightened (and could be in pain) so you will need to be tactful and sympathetic with her. You do not have much time, however, so perhaps you could carefully examine the driver of the car while you are talking to the lady.

The most important and urgent question to answer is:

Is anyone dying, or likely to die unless you give treatment?

STEP 3 – Treatment

Leading on from that last question, you must:

Give priority to the most urgent conditions.

If a person can shout (like the lady in the car) then the airway is open and the casualty can breathe. **Look for people who are silent.**

Apply A, B, C – check and, if necessary, deal with airway, breathing and circulation; then control severe bleeding.

If someone is trapped and unconscious, then keep checking the airway.

Having carried out the life-saving treatment, you can finish the rest of your diagnosis and check the level of response for each unconscious casualty. Now you are ready to give treatment which is less urgent, but remember that in this area the Emergency Services will soon arrive.

Remember, do not move casualties more than is absolutely necessary.

You could, for example, open that driver's airway (and even provide other treatment) without removing him from the car as he may have fractured his spine. You should leave it to the Emergency Services to take the person from the vehicle unless there is a danger of fire or explosion or you have to give chest compression because the person's heart has stopped. **Make certain that the head is kept steady if there is the slightest possibility of neck injury.**

Treat large wounds and fractures.

Also remember that casualties may have internal bleeding or other injuries.

Treat (and guard against) shock.

The lady in the car, for example, could need treatment for this, even though she only seems to have minor cuts and bruises.

Put the person in the correct position and make them as comfortable as possible.

Remember that the **correct** position might be exactly where the person is – without moving the casualty. In this case, however, since he is breathing, you decide to put the motorcyclist in the recovery position, but not to remove his helmet.

Calm the casualties, reduce pain, handle gently and protect from the cold and damp.

All of these helpful things will probably have been done by you as you treat each casualty – bystanders can also help, however. Someone from one of the houses in that picture could bring blankets or coats to keep the casualties warm and dry – but always remember that people should be moved as little as possible.

As a First Aider you must use your common sense.

With any accident where your help is needed:

Do not try to do too much.

Do not let people crowd round and get in the way.

Do not remove or damage clothing unless you have to.

Do not give anything to eat or drink to a casualty.

STEP 4 – Disposal

At this accident one of the bystanders has already arranged for an ambulance to come.

While you are waiting for the ambulance **you must watch and record any changes in the casualty's condition.** The motorcyclist, for example, might regain consciousness . . . but the doctors will need to know that he *was* unconscious.

Remember that your responsibility does not end until the care of the casualty has been taken over by a doctor, nurse or other responsible person and you have made your report.

SUMMARY

First Aid has four parts:

1. Assessing the situation.
2. Deciding what is wrong with the casualty (diagnosis).
3. Giving immediate and appropriate treatment (in particular apply ABC to preserve life).
4. Disposing of the casualty – to doctor, hospital or home as appropriate.

First Aid treatment is given:

- To preserve life;
- To prevent the casualty's condition from becoming worse;
- To promote recovery.

To summarize the personal qualities you will need as a First Aider, we can list eight words; You must be:

Observant

Note symptoms and signs.

Tactful

Find the history and symptoms.

Resourceful

Use whoever and whatever is at hand that can help.

Dextrous

Handle the person gently and use equipment efficiently.

Explicit

Be clear in your instructions to the casualty and/or bystanders.

Discriminating

Choose priorities.

Persevering

You must keep on trying to help the casualty.

Sympathetic

You must encourage and comfort the person.

Those eight words are part of the history of the St John Ambulance – originally they surrounded the eight pointed cross which is our emblem.

Glossary

Many words which have been unfamiliar to you are explained in the main part of this book – they are included in the index.
Other words which are sometimes used by First Aiders include:

Abdomen	The belly including the stomach, liver and intestines, etc.
Angulation	With fractures – having an angle or sharp bend where one should not be.
Allergy	An unusual reaction by the body to some foods, chemicals, insect bites, etc.
Atrium	One of the two collecting chambers of the heart.
Autonomic	The autonomic nervous system regulates and controls parts of the body which are not under voluntary control.
Bacteria	Germs – tiny organisms which cause disease.
Cerebro-spinal fluid	The fluid that bathes the brain and spinal cord.
Cerebro-spinal system	The brain, spinal cord and nerves.
Coma	A state of unconsciousness resembling heavy sleep from which one cannot be roused.
Compress	A *cold* compress is a damp, cold pad which helps to cool injuries to minimise swelling and relieve pain.
Congestion	Unusual build-up of blood in some parts of the body.
Cyanosis	Bluish colour seen in face, lips and nail-beds when the blood which is in circulation does not contain enough oxygen.
Diaphragm	A strong muscular partition which separates the chest cavity from the abdominal cavity.
Epiglottis	A flap at the base of the tongue which stops food entering the airway.

Fibrillation	A quivering of muscle fibres.
Floater	With bandages – one which is positioned depending on the site of the injury.
Groin	The crease between the top of the thigh and the belly.
Haemorrhage	Bleeding.
Ice bag	A leak-proof bag full of pieces of ice used to cool injuries to minimise swelling and relieve pain.
Incontinence	Loss of control of the bladder (or possibly bowels).
Larynx	The voice-box.
Narcotic	A substance which causes drowsiness, sleep or unconsciousness.
Neil-Robertson stretcher	A stretcher for use in cramped or confined spaces.
Radius	One of the two bones in the lower arm.
Resuscitation	The process of restoring a casualty back to life – normally by using artificial ventilation (and possibly external chest compression).
Serum	A straw-coloured liquid which is left when the rest of the blood clots.
Spasm	A sudden movement or tightening of a muscle in any part of the body.
"Sucking" wound of chest	A wound which penetrates the chest wall and air is sucked in and blown out in time with breathing.
Synovial fluid	The fluid which lubricates the joints.
Tetanus	Infection which affects muscles.
Tubular gauze	A type of bandage made of a roll of seamless gauze which is put in place with a special applicator.
Ulna	One of the two bones in the lower arm.
Ventricle	One of the two pumping chambers of the heart.

Index